Busting The
LIFE INSURANCE
Lies

38 Myths And Misconceptions
That Sabotage Your Wealth

KIM D. H. BUTLER AND JACK BURNS
WITH JAMES RANSON

Copyright © 2016 by Kim D. H. Butler and Jack Burns

All rights reserved. No part of this publication may be reproduced, distributed, or transmitted in any form or by any means, including photocopying, recording, or other electronic or mechanical methods, without the prior written permission of the publisher, except in the case of brief quotations embodied in critical reviews and certain other noncommercial uses permitted by copyright law. For permission requests, write to the publisher at the address below.

Hello@ProsperityEconomicsMovement.com

A Master Wordsmith Book

THE
MASTER WORDSMITH
Masterpiece Services for Entrepreneur Authors
www.TheMasterWordsmith.com

Published by Authors Unite

www.AuthorsUnite.com

and by Prosperity Economics Advisors

www.ProsperityEconomicsAdvisors.com

DISCOVER HOW TO BUILD WEALTH *WITHOUT* WALL STREET RISKS AND WORRIES!

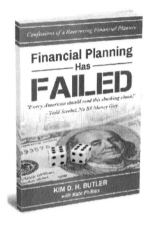

Typical financial planning is designed to make financial corporations rich, not you!

In this groundbreaking ebook, you'll discover why "typical" financial advice is flat-out wrong, and what to do with your money instead to take back control and build true wealth.

Discover "insider secrets" about lucrative investments you'll never hear about from your banker or broker. Plus, receive instant access to additional audio and video trainings on The 7 Principles of Prosperity™ with Kim Butler!

Sign up to receive *Financial Planning Has Failed* and other complimentary Prosperity Accelerator Pack resources at partners4prosperity.com/subscribe

LEARN THE WEALTH BUILDING SECRETS OF THE FAMILY RESERVE BANKING SYSTEM!

What if there was a reliable way to build tax-free, low-risk generational wealth?

There is! It's called The Family Reserve Banking System. This unique system allows you and your family to stop relying on market-based, tax-disadvantaged investments—and start building a confident financial future that spans generations.

In this free ebook, discover a way to build wealth that doesn't involve you risking your hard-earned money...and secures your future while eliminating risk and reducing your tax burden!

To get yours, visit jblife.com/subscribe

ADVISORS: BE A PART OF THE MOVEMENT AND RECEIVE A FREE COPY OF *FINANCIAL PLANNING HAS FAILED*

Enjoy Kim's story of how she abandoned her financial planning certification, left her typical financial practice, and started the Prosperity Economics Movement. This book has been ground-breaking for clients and advisors alike, showing them that we DON'T have to remain captive to Wall Street risks and a volatile stock market!

prosperity economics
ADVISORS

To discover how to stop perpetuating the half-truths of typical financial advice and start offering your clients real, sustainable solutions for wealth-building, visit ProsperityEconomicsAdvisors.com and sign up for instant access to *Financial Planning Has Failed*.

PRAISE FOR *BUSTING THE LIFE INSURANCE LIES*

"Thank-you, Jack and Kim, for cutting through the BS about life insurance! For anyone wrestling with the 'whole life vs. term insurance' and dozens of other life insurance questions, this book gives a balanced perspective from voices of experience."

Todd Strobel
No B.S. Money Guy, host of the Prosperity Podcast

"An important book for anyone who has or is considering purchasing life insurance. Cuts through the misinformation in a way that is accessible, even entertaining!"

Craig Mertz
Bank VP and CFO

"It is a breath of fresh air to see these lies 'busted' so evenhandedly... both the lies that life insurance critics tell and the lies that life insurance advisors sometimes tell (and falsely believe!) Along with Kim Butler's excellent *Live Your Life Insurance,* this book will prove invaluable for advisors and agents as well as policyholders."

Kate Phillips
Co-author of *Financial Planning Has Failed*

"Jack Burns and Kim Butler have partnered to co-author an enlightening book about a financial vehicle that should rightfully be the foundation of most families' personal economy. Best of all, it's all delivered through an engaging storytelling format that anyone can understand."

Jason Rink
Former VP at JP Morgan Chase

TABLE OF CONTENTS

Foreword by Todd Langford **16**

Introduction **18**

Meeting the Michaelsons *18*

How to use this book 20

Part 1: General Life Insurance Lies **24**

Thanksgiving Dinner at the Harding house *24*

Lie #1: Whole life insurance is a bad investment 28

Lie #2: Life insurance is like all insurance,
a necessary evil. 31

Lie #3: Store your liquid cash in a bank, not an
insurance policy 37

Lie #4: If you get life insurance, you'll end up
"insurance poor". 42

Lie #5: All life insurance companies are the same. 46

Lie #6: Life insurance advisors get paid too much 49

Lie #7: You'd do better to be self-insured by
building up your own net worth. .53

Part 2: Age, Family, and Timing Lies **58**

A family meeting 58

Lie #8: Life insurance is just for burial costs 61

Lie #9: Only people with dependents need life insurance . . .64

Lie #10: Never buy life insurance for a child 67

Lie #11: Life insurance isn't worth it when you're older 70

Lie #12: Your family doesn't need life insurance 73

Part 3: Term Life vs. Whole Life Insurance Lies **78**

The Michaelsons explore their options 78

Lie #13: Financial experts recommend AGAINST
whole life 81

Lie #14: Whole life or term? You have to pick
one or the other! 83

Lie #15: "Buy term and invest the difference" works 86

Lie #16: Whole life is too expensive and term's price
is right 89

Lie #17: The insurance company keeps your whole
life cash value when you die 92

Part 4: Payment and Money Lies **100**

The Michaelsons meet with an insurance advisor *100*

Lie #18: "Premium" means cost: you make payments
and never see your money again! 105

Lie #19: If you can't pay your premiums, you're in
serious trouble 109

Lie #20: If you borrow against your policy, you're
borrowing your own money 112

Lie #21: You have to borrow to access your money, which cuts your cash value growth .114

Lie #22: You can only count on the guaranteed column (not dividends). 117

Lie #23: Short pay policies are preferable to l onger-pay options. 121

Lie #24: You don't break even until the 20th year of paying for your policy 123

Lie #25: A whole life policy without Paid-Up Additions is worthless 125

Part 5: "Pro-whole-life" lies, the advisor's perspective, and the rest of the story **128**

Dinner with Uncle Carl *129*

Lie #26: You should put all your money into your whole life policy 137

Lie #27: A whole life policy provides regular income to fund your daily needs forever 140

Lie #28: A whole life policy means you don't need any other investments 143

Lie #29: You can borrow against your policy and never pay it back 145

Lie #30: When you borrow against a policy, you're paying interest to yourself. .148

Part 6: Advanced and technical lies for advisors and savvy clients **152**

Lie #31: Universal Life gives policyholders more flexibility and costs less 153

Lie #32: Direct recognition is bad, non-direct recognition is good. 156

Lie #33: You never want to purchase a MEC,
or let your policy become one 159

Lie #34: On a life insurance loan, you should
always pay interest in advance........................161

Lie #35: On a life insurance loan, you can choose
between simple and compound interest 162

Lie #36: You need buy-sell insurance to protect
your business 164

Lie #37: You need key person insurance, but not
personal insurance 167

Lie #38: The "gross dividend" rate equals what
you'll receive in dividends...........................169

Conclusion **172**

Illustration Appendices................................**176**

Acknowledgments.....................................**254**

About the Authors....................................**256**

About the Prosperity Economics Movement **260**

Book a Prosperity Economics Speaker..................**265**

Also by Kim D. H. Butler **268**

ILLUSTRATION APPENDICES TABLE OF CONTENTS

Illustration	Age	Lies	Page
A1 - Max PUA	10	4, 10, 22, 24	182
A2 - No PUA	10	4, 10, 22, 24	184
B1 - Fullpay + Max PUA	35	4, 14, 17, 18, 22, 23, 24	186
B2 - Max PUA, Natural Vanish	35	4, 14, 17, 18, 22, 23, 24	188
B3 - No PUA	35	4, 14, 17, 18, 22, 23, 24	190
B4 - 1-4 Yearly Renewable Term	35	4, 14, 17, 18, 22, 23, 24	192
B5 - 30 Year Level Term	35	4, 14, 17, 18, 22, 23, 24	200
C1 - Full Pay Partial PUA	50	4, 18, 22, 23, 33	202
C2 - Max PUA, Natural Vanish	50	4, 18, 22, 23, 33	204
C3 - No PUA	50	4, 18, 22, 23, 33	206
C4 - MEC	50	4, 18, 22, 23, 33	208
D1 - Death Benefit, Partial PUA	75	4, 11, 17, 22, 23, 24	210
D2 - Max PUA	75	4, 11, 17, 22, 23, 24	212
D3 - No PUA	75	4, 11, 17, 22, 23, 24	214

Illustration	Age	Lies	Page
E1 - Inforce Full Pay Male	47	19	216
E2 - Half Death Benefit Sample	47	19	220
E3 - Reduced Paid Up	47	19	222
F1 - UL "Dying on the Vine"	47	31	224
F2 - UL "Dying on the Vine"	28	31	226
G - Whole Truth Funding with Kim Butler and Todd Langford	35	1, 15, 26, 28	228

Foreword

Very few people actually know the reality of life insurance. You may be reading this book right now because you've heard unsavory things about it. You may have been told it doesn't work, it's a necessary evil, it's a "nice-to-have" but unnecessary financial option, or it's just another investment vehicle like the hundreds of others out there. You may have heard someone disparaging life insurance, especially whole life, in an online article or on a talk show. You may simply like the idea of uncovering lies in a massive industry.

But this book isn't just about pointing out lies and misconceptions. It's about using those lies to highlight a central truth: dividend-paying whole life insurance doesn't just work, it works wonders. If people truly understood the amazing benefits that come with whole life, they would be lined up around the block to buy it.

This may come as a surprise to you. It certainly did to me! I had to run a lot of calculations to make sure I was right. But the numbers don't lie. Whole life's cash value and death benefit growth most often outperform every "safe" financial vehicle out there. The rush to 401(k)s and mutual funds over the last 50-plus years has made a lot of noise and drawn a lot of positive attention away from whole life, but the truth is that whole life, with all its safety and over-150-year track record, is much more reliable than either of those vehicles.

Not only that, but most whole life companies are built to help policyholders, not shareholders. In a mutual life insurance company, all profits are paid out to policyholders as dividends. And then there's the peace of mind whole life policyholders have. They know their

Busting the Life Insurance Lies

cash value and death benefit is guaranteed to increase. They know they have immediate access to collateral and liquid funds they can use to cover costs and create opportunities. No one with a 401(k) or a mutual fund can say any of that about their money. As important as understanding the numbers are, you can't put a dollar amount on these benefits. They are literally priceless.

So if you have encountered negative talk about whole life (and I'm sure you have), I encourage you to lay aside what you've heard or read and get the real information. See for yourself if you and your family can benefit from whole life insurance...not just "someday," but while you're still living. Do your research first, without anyone's opinion, as it would be a shame to miss out on a great financial tool that could help you build more wealth with less risk.

I want to disclose that Kim Butler is my wife and Jack Burns is a colleague of both of ours. All three of us stand behind whole life completely, and are dedicated to sharing the truth of its value and power. We also (unlike many financial "professionals" out there) back up that belief with action: we own many whole life policies ourselves and use them regularly to create opportunities in our own lives.

-Todd Langford, TruthConcepts.com

Introduction

"Six cans cranberries, one bag sweet potatoes, two bags regular, four pints heavy cream, two pounds butter, half a dozen oranges for peel, and...rats, I know I'm forgetting something..." Kara Michaelson crossed her arms and glared into the open pantry.

"Is it this?" came her husband's voice, apparently catching the tail end of her thinking aloud. Kara turned to see Stephen standing at the back door, holding a large jar of mincemeat.

Kara blinked. "Um, no...since when is that on our list?"

"Since your sisters said they were only baking pumpkin pies this year. Your whole family knows I eat a few bites of pumpkin just to be polite, but this year they want to make sure I can't eat anything else."

"I'm sure they didn't mean it personally!" said Kara.

"Oh yes they did," said Stephen, closing the door and dropping a kiss on his wife's cheek. "This is a conspiracy, love. A grand conspiracy to convert me to the Harding family dessert tradition, where even my beloved mincemeat turns into a pumpkin at midnight. Well, I won't have it. I'll have mince pie if I have to bake it myself!" Stephen managed to hold a straight face for almost five seconds after this statement before he and Kara both burst out laughing.

"So if you didn't forget my mincemeat, what was it?" Stephen asked after the laughter had slackened off.

"No idea." Kara waved a dismissive hand. "It'll come back to me--probably once we're halfway there without it."

Busting the Life Insurance Lies

"That's another good reason we're driving up tonight rather than tomorrow. Grocery stores close early on Thanksgiving, if they're open at all. Tonight we can stop and get whatever it is you've forgotten." Stephen put the jar of mincemeat into the grocery bag next to the butter and cream.

"Very true," said Kara. "So what happened today?"

"Not too much. Quiet day with half the office already left for their own holidays." Stephen shrugged. "I did have an interesting talk with Dan Gordon in purchasing, remember him?"

Kara nodded. "Vaguely. What did he say?"

"He said he just got some kind of life insurance policy. I didn't understand half of what he said, but he was really excited about it. Something about being set for emergency funds and opportunities on top of the death benefit and coverage. He wants to use it to take his wife and kids to Disney next year--and apparently it's set up so he can."

"Well, that does sound pretty good. Did he say anything else about it?"

"Oh yeah, lots, not that much of it made sense to me. But it got me thinking--do you think we should look into life insurance? I mean, maybe not right this second look into it, but maybe in a year or so when you-know-who shows up?"

Kara leaned her head against his chest. She and Stephen had been trying for a baby for the last few months, but she hadn't caught yet. Stephen tightened his arms around her.

"Sorry, love. I know you're disappointed nothing's happened yet. We can talk about this later."

Kara took a deep breath and looked up at him. "No, you're right. It IS going to happen sooner or later, and life insurance might not be a bad thing to look into." She considered for a moment, unconsciously biting her lip in a way Stephen had once told her looked adorable.

"In fact, I know who we should ask about it."

"Really? Who?"

"My parents. I think they actually have a policy that's kind of like the one Dan told you about. Or at least they spent a couple months traveling last year, and I could swear I heard my dad mention something about using insurance to do it."

"Okay then, I'm sold," said Stephen. "As long as I don't have to take out a policy to make sure I get my mince pie!"

Kara swatted his arm. "Go put these bags in the car. We're out the door in thirty, buster."

Stephen winked at her, scooped up the grocery bags, and disappeared back outside.

***

There are thousands of people like Stephen and Kara. They hear about life insurance from a friend, a colleague, or even an insurance advisor. They think it's probably a good idea to look into. They decide to dig a little deeper, ask around, see what there is to see.

But then they start running into trouble.

First they hear one thing, then they hear another. Famous financial experts endorse certain kinds of insurance and disparage others-- even if the experts themselves use different insurance than they recommend. There's a lot of "they say" advice out there--and most of it is unsupported, incomplete, or just plain wrong. The media adds to this confusion by pushing the insurance agendas of whoever sponsors them. If stock brokerage companies are the sponsors--notice how much they spend on ads--of course they recommend the cheapest insurance possible so that people buy their mutual funds instead! And to make matters worse, different insurance companies and advisors give conflicting advice and recommend very different products and strategies.

Faced with all of this widely varied information, people get confused. They get frustrated. Often they go with the first thing they hear, or settle for whichever insurance policy sounds the easiest. They may even give up and forego insurance entirely.

Sadly, in doing so they lose out on the amazing benefits that getting the right life insurance can get them. They miss out on the chance to create an efficient emergency/opportunity fund that is protected for themselves and their children using life insurance.

This book is here to change that.

We've chosen to call all this confusing and variably accurate information, rumor, advice, and counsel that people run into "life insurance lies." To be clear, we don't necessarily mean "lies" to signify that anyone in the insurance industry is purposefully misleading their clients or misinforming the public. Yes, there are a few occasional bad apples (both financial advisors and life insurance agents), yet by and large, insurance advisors and companies are honest and sincere.

The problem is that in many cases, they are honestly and sincerely wrong. Even in doing their best to serve their clients, many of these people and companies are not on the right track.

So when we talk about "busting the life insurance lies," think of it like mythbusting. We believe that many of the tactics and teachings out there are incorrect and ineffective, and we're writing this book to share what we believe and have seen to work the best for the most people: whole life insurance policies. Between us, we have over fifty years of insurance experience, and we haven't seen any insurance product or strategy enrich more lives or create more peace of mind than whole life.

But as you'll see (if you don't already know), a lot of the information out there doesn't paint whole life insurance in a very good light. People say it's too complicated, too expensive, it doesn't work, its returns are too low, experts don't endorse it, there are better alternatives, etc. We don't agree with most of the criticism of whole life coming from its opponents, nor can we endorse some of the hype that sometimes comes from well-meaning salespeople. Both are usually based on misunderstandings of whole life and how it works, which we'll explain.

Whole life can create a nearly unbeatable financial foundation for many, perhaps even most people. However, it is not a magic wand that can solve all financial problems for everyone. We hope to show you that if you want a real life insurance strategy for security, peace of mind, financial flexibility and even long-term prosperity, whole life deserves serious consideration and may be exactly what works best for you.

To help show how whole life can work with real people (and to demonstrate how real people can dig through all the lies surrounding it), we've designed this book around the story of a young American couple and their family. Different family members have different thoughts and opinions about insurance, and as the young couple you just met looks into their own insurance situation, they'll run into many of the lies we want to bust. So as you enjoy Stephen and Kara's story, you can also enjoy seeing how each myth you may have encountered around life insurance falls away.

Busting the Life Insurance Lies

To get the most out of the story, we recommend reading the book all the way through, but if you see a particular lie you want to look up immediately, go right ahead.

One quick note on word choice: when we use the term "advisor," we mean a life insurance advisor, preferably one who specializes in whole life. We chose this term over the other common term, "agent," because that term has far stronger negative connotations than "advisor" does, and because most people working in life insurance do call themselves "advisors" these days. We caution readers, however, not to confuse a life insurance advisor with a financial advisor. Financial advisors, as the financial services industry calls them, are more often really investment advisors, and are rarely versed in life insurance at all. In fact, financial advisors tend to be some of the people most likely to tell you a life insurance lie! So please be aware of our meaning when we talk about "advisors" throughout this book.

Finally, it's our pleasure to be sharing our experiences and perspectives with you in these pages. We've both spent many years in the insurance industry, and we've seen firsthand what a helpful, transforming, even life-saving effect whole life insurance can have on the lives of its policyholders and their families. We aren't just here because our industry gets a bad rep, or because people are being misinformed. We're here to help you. It is our hope that this book will alleviate your confusion and frustration around the life insurance industry once and for all--and more, that it will help set you on a path of financial freedom and peace of mind.

Thanks for reading!

Kim Butler and Jack Burns

Part 1:

GENERAL
LIFE INSURANCE LIES

THANKSGIVING DAY

Clang! Clang! Clang!

Kara loved that her parents had an actual dinner bell, even if it only ever got rung on holidays, when there were enough kids around to argue over who got to ring it. It had only been a decade or so since she'd been one of the older kids who claimed that right by seniority herself.

Her mom leaned around the kitchen door jamb. "Better move, K. You're standing in the prime traffic path!"

"Oh, I know!" Kara said, stepping quickly into the kitchen as a tide of jersey-clad men and boys began tramping through the hallway she'd just occupied on the way to the dining room. It was Thanksgiving Day, after all, and there were at least three different football games on.

Kara liked football herself, but she'd opted to help her mom, sisters, and various other family members with the morning's cooking to try and snag a few moments to share her hopes that she and Stephen might be expecting soon. Unfortunately, the moment hadn't materialized until now.

"Mom? Got a second?" she said as she realized she and her mom were finally the only two people in the kitchen.

Kara's mother, Liza Harding, was the image of everyone's favorite grandmother. Kara knew this because on more than one occasion, her nieces and nephews had pointed out that the drawings of kindly grandmothers in different children's books looked a lot like their Grandma--silver hair in a wispy bun, red cheeks, sparkling eyes and all. Liza dusted flour from her hands and looked at her youngest daughter. "Of course, K, if you'll help me carry these dishes in."

Kara nodded and picked up several serving bowls. "Stephen and I have been trying to get pregnant," she said quickly.

Liza smiled. "That's grand, honey. I love the grandkids I have, but you know I'll never say no to more!"

"Well, nothing's happened yet."

"It will. Are you nervous?"

"A little," Kara admitted. "We were hoping to catch by now." Now that she had her mom's ear, she found she didn't want to talk about how she felt after all--not while carrying dishes, anyway. "We were, um, talking about life insurance yesterday," she went on. "You and Dad have that, right?"

"We certainly do, K. How do you think your father and I go on our cruises every year?"

"I don't get it. How does insurance pay for--"

But Kara was interrupted by the stampede of kids running in from ringing the dinner bell. In moments, everyone was crowded around the dining room table and adjacent kids' table, grace had been said, and dishes were passing back and forth.

Kara found herself sitting a few places away from her father. "Dad," she called across two cousins, "I was asking Mom about life insurance just now, but we got interrupted. How does yours work?"

"Oh no, not insurance!" groaned one of the cousins in between them before Bill Harding could answer his youngest daughter. "As if we didn't have enough to spend money on already!"

"Right?" put in the other cousin. "And you gotta pay so much to it, it's a wonder you've got any left to live on. I know a guy who only eats ramen because he's got such high premiums to pay. Imagine having to live on ramen because of insurance! It's ridiculous."

Noticing both cousins shoveling down stuffing and mashed potatoes as if facing a three-month famine, Kara doubted either of them could actually imagine living on ramen. She very carefully did not say this out loud. Instead, she looked past them to her dad again. "Dad?"

"Well, K, we have a policy called a whole life insurance policy. It's--"

"Say, don't those policies have terrible returns?" This came from Kara's brother-in-law, Chad, sitting across the table from her. "I hear the way to go is to invest, make a bundle for yourself, and then bam, you're set for life. You don't need insurance when you've got money invested!"

"You sure about that, honey?" asked his wife, Kara's second-oldest sister Jeanne. "I thought the safest place for money is in a bank. That's got to be way better than an insurance policy, anyway."

"Make more money investing, but yeah, sure, both are better than

insurance," Chad said around a mouthful of turkey. "All the insurance companies are the same: out to take your money. Why do you think they get such big commissions?" There was general nodding in response to this declaration. Kara noticed her father didn't join in.

"What do you think, Dad?" she pressed on, silencing one of the cousins with a glare when he attempted to interject again.

"Well, K, I think this dinner table's a terrible place to tell you what I think. It'd take me till dessert just to respond to what everyone's just brought up, let alone tell you what your mom and I use and why. Why don't we do this: tomorrow morning, after the kids go out sledding, let's you and me and your mother and Stephen refill our coffee and talk about it then."

"Can I join in? I'm interested, too," came a deeper voice from her dad's other side. Kara craned her neck to see, and recognized Victor, her oldest sister Elaine's boyfriend of three years.

"Sure!" boomed Bill. "The more, the merrier! I'll bring the cinnamon rolls."

***

As Grandpa Bill pointed out, the various cousins, sisters, and brothers-in-law brought up several life insurance lies. We like to call these "general lies," since they tend to relate to life insurance in a broad, nonspecific way. They don't have to do with types of policy, size of premiums, expert recommendations, or anything like that--they just show some people's knee-jerk reasons to dismiss life insurance out of hand.

Let's take a look at these general lies here before we rejoin Kara at tomorrow morning's Insurance Info Family Meeting.

Lie #1:
WHOLE LIFE INSURANCE IS A BAD INVESTMENT

Probably the first and loudest lie we hear is that whole life is a lousy investment opportunity. People say this one all kinds of different ways:

- The rate of return is poor, I can do better investing elsewhere.

- If I buy life insurance I'll lose out because I can't invest elsewhere.

- I have to die to get any value out of life insurance, so I'll invest elsewhere.

When people hear statements like these, they tend to jump ship and pursue other investments...without actually checking to see if any of them are true or not. And they end up missing out on all the huge advantages that come with whole life.

First of all, we don't feel like whole life should be called an investment in the first place, because it really isn't one. It doesn't actually invest in any market, it isn't dependent on stock market swings, it doesn't require a broker or financial advisor to manage it, it has much better liquidity and accessibility, it's much more likely to pay dividends, it provides a death benefit, its fee structure is very different, its growth is tax-deferred as long as it stays in the policy...the list of differences goes on.

Busting the Life Insurance Lies

A whole life policy is not an investment, but it IS an asset of the highest quality. It's a place to store liquid cash that also provides immediate protection benefits. It's permanent life insurance, AND it's the best long-term savings vehicle we know of. Not only does calling it a bad investment belie its relatively strong rate of eventual return, calling it an investment at all creates confusion around what whole life is, why you'd use it, and how to compare it to its alternatives.

Now about that return: if the rate of return is bad...compared to what? Once a whole life policy gets some cash value built up, its annual rate of return (AROR) actually rises higher than most liquid vehicles' rates ever will (savings accounts and money markets). The growth of cash value inside whole life policies settles at about 3.5-5% (depending on age, health, and other factors) as of this writing in 2016. (You can ask your advisor to calculate your policy's exact rate--it changes each year depending on dividends.)

Now, 3.5-5% may not impress you, but understand that cash value is a liquid, tax-advantaged asset that can never drop in value, like so many other investments. Taking the midrange of 4%, it is actually better than anything you'd get with typical liquid accounts like money market accounts (currently 0.2%) and treasury bills (currently 1.7%). And it's much better than a bank savings account's return--as of this writing, bank interest rates are sitting just above zero. So with time, the return on whole life becomes stronger than many other options. (For a visual calculator comparing life insurance to an "alternate" account, see Appendix G.)

Plus, don't overlook the death benefit! This is an immense "return" that a whole life policy gives immediately and permanently as soon as you pay the first premium. Too often, self-proclaimed financial experts, gurus and bloggers neglect to include the death benefit at all when comparing whole life with other assets. Of course, this skews the numbers significantly! A death benefit provides significant additional value to your estate over and above the cash value you will build over time.

There's nothing wrong with a diverse investment portfolio--we're not saying insurance and investing are mutually exclusive or that you should do only one at the expense of the other. If you have the resources to do both, by all means do both. In fact, a whole life policy can actually help you invest. Some advisers recommend whole life as a highly effective diversification strategy that can strengthen overall returns and safety while making distributions from market-based retirement accounts more efficient. (After all, you don't want to have to liquidate stocks when they're down, do you?)

You can also use your cash value as collateral for another investment, or you can lean on it as a safety net if you run into any investment issues. For instance, real estate investors have a high need for liquidity for repairs, vacancies, and down payments on new properties. Whole life is a fantastic place to grow and keep cash that can be easily borrowed against.

This is why whole life insurance is an "and" asset, meaning you can have cash value for emergencies or opportunities and use it to invest in other things. Compare that to a 401(k) or 403(b) retirement plan as an example. We call those "or" assets, because you can either invest in them, *or* you can keep your cash liquid. With these products, you're essentially putting your money in a box and throwing away the key. Try to get anything out of a 401(k) or IRA before age 59½, and you'll likely pay significant penalties. This is why, if you only have the funds for insurance or investing, we'd recommend starting with insurance. You'll want to build your savings and emergency fund first so that you don't end up liquidating investments for car repairs or medical bills.

Busting the Life Insurance Lies

Not only should you start saving BEFORE you invest, but you may also want to put some protection in place, especially if you have a spouse or any dependents. This is another way that whole life is an "and" asset...you'll be protecting your income while you're saving for the future!

Finally, if you've been wary of life insurance because you've heard that you have to die before you get any value, hopefully you now understand this is not true. While many investment products (even good ones) are designed so that you DON'T have access to your money, whole life is just the opposite. It's a financial foundation that is designed to be used...*your whole life*.

If there's one thing we'd like you to take away from this book, it's that life insurance is a tool for improving your life, not just covering for your death. No financial vehicle is as useful as whole life for emergencies, opportunities, investments, for providing your own financing, permanent protection for your earning capability, or for your peace of mind.

Lie #2:
LIFE INSURANCE IS LIKE ALL INSURANCE, A NECESSARY EVIL

Okay, let's face it: sometimes insurance feels a lot like taxes. It's a necessary evil, something you're supposed to pay for (or required to pay for) but that you'd really rather not spend good money on. When you're already paying health insurance, car insurance, renter's or homeowner's insurance, and so on, adding life insurance can seem like just one more extra expense.

Plus, somewhere along the way life insurance started to mean "death insurance" for most people. So to add insult to injury, now life insurance makes people think about death and taxes. No wonder they don't like dealing with it.

So really there are two lies here: first, that life insurance is like all other insurance; and second, that it's something you *should* have, but don't really *want* to have.

First things first. While life insurance has some things in common with other forms of insurance--the monthly or annual premium, for starters--there's one monumental difference between life insurance and every other kind of insurance. Life insurance covers something that is guaranteed to happen. As a pastor in St. Louis, MO, once said: the human death rate, statistically, hovers right around 100%.

So while car insurance covers an "if" event ("if" you get in an accident), health insurance covers an "if" event ("if" you get sick), and

Busting the Life Insurance Lies

other types of insurance also cover "if" events ("if" your basement floods, "if" there's a fire, "if" your house is burgled, etc.), life insurance is unique in covering a "when" event: *when* you die. Whether that happens next week, next year, or 50+ years from now doesn't matter. Of course, we all hope it's the third choice! But even if it isn't, a whole life insurance policy will provide a benefit to your survivors and heirs no matter when you pass.

This is huge, for two reasons. One is that you can't remove or reduce your need for life insurance by being a safe driver or living a healthy life; you may die later, but you'll still die. The other is that because life insurance is based on the end of your life, it actually allows you to change how you'll live in the years before that end.

Which brings us to the second lie here, that you technically ought to have life insurance, but it's not something you really want. This is possibly the biggest myth about life insurance we encounter. For most people who actually have it, whole life insurance is a wonderful and joyous thing that makes their lives easier, happier, and more peaceful. Because in reality, life insurance is not something for dying but something for living.

We talked in lie #1 about borrowing against your whole life insurance policy's cash value as a better option than borrowing from a bank or withdrawing money from your bank account. What we didn't talk about then, but want to introduce now, is the second part of that point: borrowing against a whole life insurance policy is the best tool we've found for improving the quality of your life.

Let's say you want to buy a new piece of equipment for your business, a $20,000 cost. A bank will charge you 21% interest on the loan or lease for that equipment, even if you prepay the lease--a hefty chunk of change. But if you borrow against your whole life policy, you'll only need to pay 5-8% interest to the insurance company, a rate spread of 13% or more that will ultimately save you over $4,000 (see calculator).

We like to call this "being your own bank," and it's just one of many ways the collateral of your whole life policy's cash value can open up opportunities and allow you to do things you wouldn't be able to otherwise.

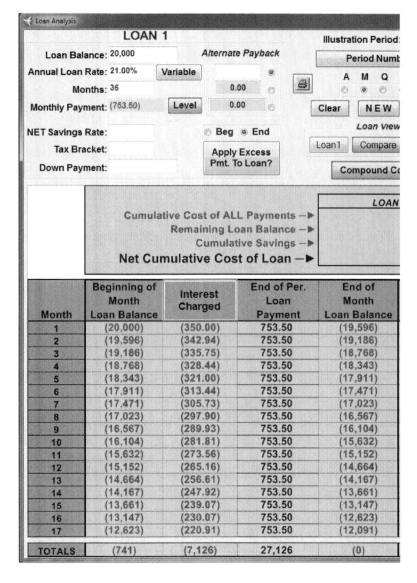

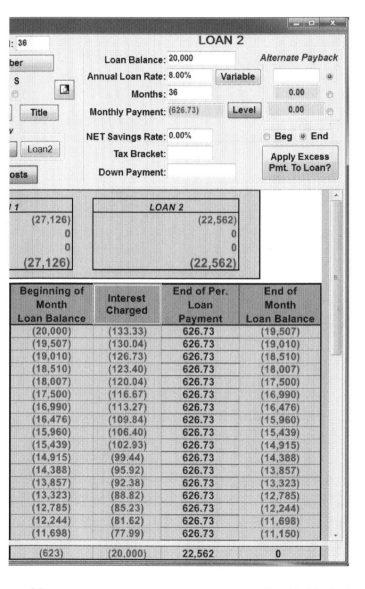

It doesn't only work with business expenses, either. As long as you can repay the loan, there's no restrictions on what you use that cash for. Business investments, new income streams, a college education, a new roof for your house, even a dream vacation or a new car-- no one but you gets to decide whether your reason for borrowing is valid or not. And since you're borrowing against the cash value rather than withdrawing funds, that cash value remains the same and continues growing no matter how much you borrow.

This is the real reason life insurance isn't a necessary evil, something you have to pay into but won't get anything out of because you'll be dead. Instead, it's a long-term savings plan that will allow you to live a richer and happier life, while providing a legacy for the people and causes that you care about. That all adds up to peace of mind, and we think that's pretty priceless.

Lie #3:
YOU SHOULD STORE YOUR LIQUID CASH IN A BANK, NOT A LIFE INSURANCE POLICY

When you think of money, you think of banks. It's one of those associations that gets ingrained into your mind as you grow up. For food you go to a grocery store, for mail you go to a post office, for anything dealing with money you go to a bank. It's just what you do. Probably the only time you've ever thought putting your money in a bank was a bad thing was when you first watched *Mary Poppins,* and wanted little Michael Banks to be able to spend his tuppence on feeding the birds instead of giving it to the crotchety old bank manager to deposit.

So when you think about saving money, your first instinct is to put it in a bank. And that's okay. Storing your money in a bank isn't a bad option. But it's not necessarily the best option. For one thing, there are a number of issues around bank accounts that many people aren't aware of; for another, there are several ways that a whole life insurance policy can be a better place to store your cash.

The first thing to understand about a bank account is that the account itself is also the bank's asset. That means that they get more of the benefit of having that value on their balance sheet than you do. This may not seem like a big deal--after all, it's still your money and you can access it any time you want--but it becomes a lot more important when you consider the concept of collateral.

Collateral, as you probably know, is the term for assets that you can use to secure a loan or investment. The value of the collateral assets tells your lender or broker that you're good for the money you want to borrow. The thing is, people typically don't use their bank accounts as collateral. Most people just withdraw their money instead. But many people do borrow against their life insurance policies, since borrowing doesn't decrease the policies' cash value--and withdrawing money does. We'll talk more about how that works in a later lie, but for now, note that using a life insurance policy as collateral makes much more sense than using a bank account, not least because the policy is your asset, not the insurance company's asset.

Now what about safety? The other big argument in favor of storing money in banks is that it's completely safe. Consumer deposits are insured up to $250,000 by the FDIC, banks seem to have great security (you almost never hear about one getting robbed anymore), and the banking industry has gone to great lengths to gain and hold the public's trust. Even if a savings account isn't a great asset, at least it's safe, right?

So far, yes. But the crash of 2008 and the subsequent bank bailouts have severely shaken that trust in banking. In that crash, only stockholders lost their money, not account holders or clients. But those stockholders lost a lot of money. The banks that managed their investments required billions of dollars from the government just to stay solvent.

And that's just in the US. Look at the banking failures in Europe. In mid-2015, Greece's banks were essentially frozen for several weeks, allowing the Greek people to withdraw only rationed amounts of money each day--no matter how much they had deposited. At the time of this writing, that country's financial crisis still hasn't been completely solved.

Busting the Life Insurance Lies

These circumstances may mean little or nothing for your personal deposits right now, but some experts aren't so sure your money will be safe in the case of another crash. Ellen Brown, author of *Web of Debt* and *The Public Bank Solution,* noted in late 2014 that the amount of federal money available to insure consumer deposits is only a fraction of the money all consumers have deposited: $46 billion in the FDIC reserve vs. $4.5 trillion in aggregated deposits. The FDIC is a good counter to a bank occasionally being robbed... but if all the banks collapse at once, their reserve won't come close to covering the amounts deposited.

Not only that, but the same banks holding that $4.5 trillion in deposits are also responsible for over $280 trillion in derivatives (securities dependent on the value of underlying assets like bonds, stocks, commodities, and interest rates). Brown points out that under 2005's bankruptcy reform act, banks are responsible for derivatives before client deposits. In other words, if another crash happened, insolvent banks could legally take those deposits--your hard-earned money-- to cover their derivative losses. Brown and others have called this potentiality a "bail-in," since the money that keeps banks from insolvency will come from their biggest creditors: depositors like you and me.

How likely is this to happen? Depending on who you ask, it could be anywhere from a slim chance to inevitable. We don't know for sure, and this isn't a financial forecasting book. But what we do know is that if banks are being revealed as much more vulnerable than we've traditionally thought, it might be worth storing your money elsewhere. And since the 2008 crash was closely tied to the stock and real estate markets, while life insurance has no ties to those markets, a whole life policy might actually turn out to be much safer than a bank account.

Finally, even if a bank doesn't end up taking your money, you still could lose it from your bank account. Under civil asset forfeiture laws, federal, state, and local governments can view and track the money in your bank account, and so can the IRS. If any of those bodies suspect you may be engaged in illegal activity, they can freeze your accounts and seize your money without any proof or evidence that you've committed a crime, or even accusing you of anything. In fact, the burden of proof will be on you to show that you were completely above board, and *even if you do prove your innocence,* you may not get your money back.

One of the more public examples of civil forfeiture happened in 2012. Early that year, three brothers named Hirsch had the bank accounts for their Long Island, NY, distribution company frozen and $447,000 confiscated by the federal government, without ever being accused of a crime or presented with evidence of wrongdoing. They did eventually get the money back, but only after three years, tens of thousands in legal fees (which they didn't get back), and ultimately the threat of bad publicity for the soon-to-be new US Attorney General, Loretta Lynch, whose office was prosecuting the case. Hundreds of others haven't been so lucky, and have given up on ever getting their money back.

The chances you will be subject to civil asset forfeiture is pretty small. But the bigger issue here isn't how many people have to deal with that--it's whether anyone, government or otherwise, has the power to oversee, and potentially take, your money. If that money is in a bank account, sadly, those authorities do have that power.

If it's in an insurance policy, they usually don't. The growth on your cash value in your whole life insurance policy doesn't get reported to the IRS. Your cash value doesn't need to be included on asset reports or FAFSA student aid applications. Borrowing against your policy's cash value doesn't need a credit check or even go on your credit report. The money in your life insurance policy is totally protected from creditors in many states and partially protected in others, on top of being a private account in general. So if the privacy of your money is important to you, a whole life policy might be a better option for you than a bank account.

Okay, we realize that this lie is kind of a downer. And we're not trying to scare you into (or out of) anything. But because the bank vs. policy argument is one of the first ones people usually encounter, we decided to hit it hard near the front of the book and get it out of the way. To soften the blow a bit, here's a more fun note on banks: did you know they buy insurance policies themselves? Yep, you read that right. Banks often use their profits and/or operating capital (much of which comes from investments they make with your deposited money) to buy insurance policies to fund their employee benefits, or sometimes to increase their liquidity. If the banks themselves are buying policies with your money, doesn't it make sense to consider using that money on a policy for yourself instead?

Lie #4:
IF YOU GET LIFE INSURANCE, YOU'LL END UP "INSURANCE POOR"

The term "insurance poor" is actually a way to describe being over-insured, where you are paying for so much insurance that you don't have enough money left over to live on (and apparently end up eating ramen). It's a common argument against taking out a life insurance policy.

Like many pervasive lies, this one has a couple grains of truth to it. For one thing, in the US we all need (and are often legally required to have) several different kinds of insurance: health insurance, car insurance if we drive, homeowner's or renter's insurance for where we live, etc. So when we look at life insurance, it's easy to think "don't I already pay enough for that? The last thing I need is *more* insurance!"

Also, for the first few years of funding a life insurance policy, cash value builds up slowly, so it can feel like you're paying premiums but not getting much return yet. When you add that payment to your other regular expenses, it can definitely feel like you're suddenly poor, or even that you might have to choose between paying your premium and paying for something else you need. So at first glance, the "insurance poor" lie may not seem like a lie at all.

Here's one big reason that it actually is one: life insurance is an *asset*, not an *expense*. And premiums, even the early ones, build cash value for you. This money that you pay into it turns into savings over time. Eventually you'll make back everything you paid in premiums, and then some, in the cash value of your policy. To see what that can look like, see Appendices A, B, C and D.

So while you may feel poorer in the short term, you are actually building wealth in the long term. If you approach life insurance from the perspective of building an asset, it may be easier not to feel "insurance poor."

That being said, there's a big difference between having as much insurance *as you can afford* and having so much insurance that you can't pay for anything else. This difference is likely the real root of the "insurance poor" lie. Many people believe the life insurance industry tells them to fund their future at the expense of their present, to pay lots of money now (no matter their financial situation) to cover an event that probably won't happen for forty years or more. They feel like they'll be pushed to spend money they may not have on something they may not need for a long time. And sadly, there have been many unethical and unscrupulous advisors whose actions have given some validation to that belief.

If you're one of these people, we hear you. We understand it can be difficult to trust an industry that seems to push you to spend more money than you're comfortable with on something you may not feel is immediately important. We get that building a wealth asset for your future doesn't do you any good if you can't pay for your life now. And we don't support any advisor who tells you otherwise or pushes you to do anything you don't want to do.

But we also think there's a better way to think about life insurance than being afraid of paying too much for it.

First of all, approaching life insurance as an asset you'll be building over time, as noted above, can help. But you don't have to feel like you need to start building it today, or else you'll miss out on some intangible but vitally important benefit. (That's actually a whole other lie in and of itself, which we'll talk about in section 2 of this book.) Start a whole life insurance policy when it makes sense for you to start one: when you have the money to pay the premiums. If you struggle to pay your bills month to month now, getting a whole life insurance policy on top of those bills will almost certainly lead to your feeling "insurance poor."

If you're trying to lose weight, there's one diet or exercise program that will almost always work: *the one you actually follow*. If you're building a business, there's one business plan that usually leads to success: *the one you actually implement*. And in life insurance, there's one policy that is most likely to set you up for security and prosperity: *the one you are actually able to fund*. So if you need a year or two to get your finances to a better level before starting your policy, by all means take that time. Life insurance isn't going anywhere. It'll be ready when you are.

That being said, if there are people who depend on your income right now, you might need to get a policy in place to protect and provide for them--whether you're ready or not. If whole life is out of reach in this scenario, you can look for a term life insurance policy instead. Term life policies only last for a short time, hence their name (usually a term of 1-30 years), but because they expire and give no benefit after that term ends, their premiums are much lower than whole life's premiums. Term is statistically worse than whole life in the long run, for a lot of reasons (we'll talk more about term vs. whole in section 3 of this book), but it is cheaper, it gets you an immediate death benefit, and sometimes it can be converted to whole life later on.

Finally, if you do feel ready for a whole life insurance policy but are still concerned about the high initial premiums, there are a number of ways you can adjust some of your other insurance payments and/ or expenses to help make up for the new cost. For instance:

Busting the Life Insurance Lies

- If your health or car insurance policies have a high premium and a lower deductible, consider switching to higher-deductible policies with lower monthly payments. Psychologically this may feel counterintuitive, but if you don't use those policies often (say, for regular medical needs), you will most likely save money by doing this.

- Make sure you're not insuring anything twice. For example, you don't need an AAA membership if your car insurance policy already covers towing services. And you don't need special life insurance for a certain disease if you have whole life insurance that will pay regardless.

- If you have or are considering starting an emergency fund, consider making your whole life insurance policy your emergency fund. Unlike a bank account, in an emergency you can borrow against your policy's cash value without draining money out of it, making emergency response more secure and easier to recover from. If you're regularly putting money away for the proverbial rainy day, you can divert that money to cover some or all of your insurance premiums.

This lie is partly a question of managing financial resources. No one's ever said they were 401(k) poor, or mutual fund poor, or vacation home poor...but most of the people who invest in those vehicles do it because they don't have to decide between investing and paying their car payment. They already have enough money to do both.

Life insurance is not an investment vehicle, but in this case the same logic applies: being "insurance poor" doesn't come from getting life insurance at all, it comes from spending money on life insurance that you also need to spend on living. Life insurance will help you improve your financial situation in the medium and long terms. But if you can't afford it in the short term right now, it's okay to wait until you can.

Lie #5:
ALL LIFE INSURANCE COMPANIES ARE THE SAME

This lie is actually two lies in one: "insurance companies are interchangeable," and "insurance companies all want the same thing: my money." As with the insurance poor lie, it's easy to think that all life insurance companies are the same or are just in it for the money *when you don't understand the industry yet.* Since you're reading this book, you clearly want to understand life insurance, which means you won't want to lump all companies and policies into the same bucket. And while there are some similarities between companies, there are also many differences.

First of all, not all companies offer the same types of life insurance. If you're looking for a particular type of life insurance, like whole life, check and see that the companies you're interested in actually have what you want--because not all life insurance companies provide whole life.

There's also the difference between mutual companies and stock companies. Mutual companies are owned by the policyholders, who have voting rights regarding the board members who manage the company, and are required by law to return all of their profits to the policyholders in the form of a dividend. That is, with these companies, your policy actually pays you. If receiving a dividend in addition to growing your cash value on a guaranteed basis is an important feature for you, a mutual company is the way to go.

Busting the Life Insurance Lies

46

Stock companies, on the other hand, are owned by shareholders and their goal is to maximize shareholder value. They are beholden to both policyholders and shareholders, meaning they have to pay two different groups of people with two different sets of priorities. This tends to lead to much less stability. Does the old adage "you can't serve two masters" ring a bell?

There are hybrids of mutual and stock companies, called mutual holding companies. As you might expect, they are more stable than stock companies, but not quite as beneficial to the policyholders as mutual companies. (Note: having the word "mutual" in its name doesn't automatically make an insurance company a mutual company. Liberty Mutual, for instance, is a stock company. Similarly, not all mutual companies have that word in their names, either.)

From our research over many years, we've determined that most whole life policies from mutual companies are very similar. There may be a few differences in policy rules from one company to the next, but for the most part, *over the long term,* all whole life policies from mutual, participating (dividend-paying) companies perform pretty much the same. So since you'll be getting essentially the same policy everywhere you look, which *person* helps you get that policy becomes more important than which company.

It's a little like going out for a good cheeseburger. You don't just get your cheeseburger at Red Robin or Fuddrucker's over Steak N Shake or Whataburger, say, because of the burger itself. You may like the actual cheeseburger better at one burger joint or another, but at the end of the day they're all cheeseburgers. (Unless you're going to In'N'Out Burger, of course, in which case the Double-Double cheeseburger really is the best.) What usually really matters is the kind of *restaurant experience* you want to have. If you want a leisurely, family-friendly dinner place where the staff sings to you on your birthday, Red Robin's got you covered, but if you only need a quick bite on the way back from a late night out, Whataburger is probably the better choice.

In the same way, when you're shopping for a whole life policy, you want to focus on who is helping you (the individual agent or advisor) and what you want to do with the policy (your strategy) over and above the policy itself. Your life insurance policy will be with you for a long time. You don't want to be stuck with an advisor that you just don't get along with on a human level. Choose an advisor you feel comfortable with and that you can trust. If you don't feel like you can have a conversation with or ask (and get answers to) honest questions of your advisor and other people in the company, it probably won't be the right company for you.

Lie #6:
LIFE INSURANCE ADVISORS GET PAID TOO MUCH

This lie is an alternate phrasing of "they're only after my money." It's easy to believe this particular lie, because insurance advisors typically work on commission. So whenever an advisor describes or recommends a particular policy or product, the buyer tends to think the advisor is pushing the one with the biggest commission, not necessarily the right one for the buyer.

Unfortunately, there are a few unscrupulous advisors who have done exactly this. They've pushed pricier policies to get bigger commissions, or conveniently failed to educate clients on useful policy add-ons that don't pay commissions themselves (like Paid-Up Additions, a very helpful but commission-free rider which we'll talk about in several later lies). Plus, compared to financial planners and stockbrokers, insurance advisors do appear to get ridiculous commission rates. So while this lie is definitely a lie, it's one that's very easy to fall for if you don't know the truth--or don't understand, as most people don't, how insurance commissions actually work and how they compare with fees on other assets over time.

First of all, the cost of an advisor's commission is already built into the policy itself, so you're not paying anything extra for the advisor's services no matter what kind of policy you get. And no matter how big the commission is, the advisor still needs to sell a lot of policies to make their living, so any one policy won't have any more effect on their income than any other policy of commensurate value. Not to mention the fact that the government regulates life insurance fees and commissions. A life insurance advisor would lose their license, and possibly go to jail, if they were caught overcharging clients.

Also, you're probably aware that fees paid on investment vehicles like 401(k)s or mutual funds are calculated based on *the total value of your account*. So even if it seems like you're paying a small percentage, the fee grows as your money grows, eventually becoming way more than you bargained for. Because life insurance and investing are often (incorrectly) lumped together, many people believe that life insurance commissions work the same way. They don't. Life insurance has a totally different method for charging fees, calculating the advisor's commission based on the money you'll put in that year alone, not the total account value. So even if you have a policy valued at multiple millions of dollars, you won't pay your advisor's commission based on that seven-figure value.

Let's look at an example. Say a 35-year-old policyholder gets a $1,000,000 death benefit policy with a $10,000 annual premium. The typical advisor commission for that is around $6,000. That's 60% of the premium amount, which seems huge! But compared to the value of the asset itself (the one-million-dollar policy), that commission is actually not 60% or even 6%, but 0.6%. That's a much better percentage--and, as we'll see shortly, a much better deal than the investment alternatives offer.

So the life insurance advisor gets their $6,000 out of the first $10,000 premium (which is likely where the myth that the advisor gets paid too much comes from, as well as the sub-myth that the advisor gets the entire first premium, which is sometimes the case but not always). They'll also receive renewals (fees awarded when a policy is renewed) over the next nine years of the policy, which usually add up to the same as their initial commission. Here's what renewals typically look like:

- Year 2: $ 1000
- Year 3: $ 1000
- Year 4: $ 800
- Year 5: $ 800
- Year 6: $ 600
- Year 7: $ 600
- Year 8: $ 400
- Year 9: $ 400
- Year 10: $ 400
- Total: $ 6000

Each of those is a small fraction of the premium amount. 0.6% up front, and another 0.6% amortized (spread out) over the next nine years, to create a one-million-dollar (and growing!) asset for you and your family.

Building a $1M death benefit immediately for just over 1% total commission is a fantastic deal! Compare that to a realtor, who would take 5% or 6% of the selling price--$50K or $60K on a $1M house. Same with a stockbroker: remember, they might only charge a 1% fee, but since they'd charge that fee on the full account balance year after year, they'd clear $100,000 in this same timeframe. (Then they'll take $10k+ each and every year after that!) As noted above, the broker or financial advisor does the exact opposite of what the life insurance advisor does: the insurance advisor gets a bigger fee up front that tapers off immediately, while the broker gets a tiny amount up front that grows immensely over time. Which of those would you prefer?

Tom Dyson, a friend and colleague of ours, once interviewed an insurance advisor who calmly stated that he took the entire first year's payment as commission. Tom was somewhat alarmed at that, until he did some more research and realized that the huge up front payment tapered off to nothing within a few years. Contrasting that with asset manager fees that start out small and grow as your investment grows, Tom realized the truth behind this lie: most people think insurance commissions are too high because they only look at one year. (You can read Tom's whole report on this event in the article "Insurance Commission Shock" on Partners4Prosperity.com.)

Remember, this policy is a long-term wealth-building asset. A few commission dollars up front are a small price to pay for a secure and prosperous financial life, right? We certainly think so. Besides, wouldn't you rather have a highly-paid surgeon perform your procedure than a poorly paid one? The same follows for life insurance advisors.

Finally, most advisors really do have your best interests at heart. They want to get to know you and your desires and find the strategy that works best for you. For many advisors, life insurance is a passion that flows from a desire to help others. A good advisor will have no problem answering your questions and explaining their recommendations to you.

If your life insurance advisor suggests a more expensive policy, ask them why they think this policy suits you best. Don't just assume that they are trying to get a better commission. It may really be the right policy for you--and if they're an honest advisor, they'll be able to tell you with sincerity why they think so.

Lie #7:
I'D DO BETTER TO BE SELF-INSURED BY INVESTING AND BUILDING UP MY OWN NET WORTH

This lie comes from a fairly obvious statement: if you're rich, you can pay for almost anything. Very few problems remain problematic after you throw a few thousand dollars at them. And much like we think of banks when we think of storing money, we also tend to think of investing when we think of growing money.

So the idea of self-insurance by simply making a lot of money and then investing it has a natural appeal. When combined with other life insurance lies that brokers and financial advisors often use (whole life is an inefficient use of resources, it gets low returns, you can do better on your own, etc.), this idea has done a lot to perpetuate the recent rush away from life insurance and toward investment vehicles like mutual funds, money market accounts, annuities, and other stock-market-based investments. But this strategy makes a lot of faulty assumptions around what you'll be able to do with those investments, not to mention incorrectly representing what life insurance does and doesn't do.

Self-insurance looks like this: build up a sizable reserve of personal investment assets (and possibly liquid cash) to protect yourself financially, and use it as a cushion, fallback, or stopgap when the going gets tough. If your home is destroyed in a natural disaster, your stockpile of money would allow you to rebuild the home yourself without needing to deal with the bureaucracy of home insurance companies, government disaster aid, and so on. Medical emergencies and treatments, accidents, even thefts become areas you resolve with your own money when you self-insure.

But there are several major problems with self-insurance. First, not everyone can even do it. Insurance premiums may be pricey, but they're nothing compared with the kind of cash you need to come up with to self-insure through investing. And what about in the meantime, while you're growing your investments? What happens if they don't grow fast enough for you to self-insure before your term insurance runs out, or you are diagnosed with something that prevents you from getting life insurance later?

Self-insurance through getting rich is most often recommended by people who are already rich, or at least who have been able to put away some money on top of their living costs. But for millions of other people, self-insurance just isn't an option no matter how hard they work. There's a big difference between earning enough to live on and building long-term wealth. Most families who can't afford to self-insure will be financially wiped out when death or disaster strikes--unless they have real insurance.

Second, having a large net worth or a strong pool of assets doesn't guarantee that you'll be safe and solvent the rest of your life, or that your loved ones will be provided for after you pass. The uncomfortable truth is that investments can and do fail. In fact, it's almost inevitable that an investment will suffer or fall through at some point, putting you back to square one with very little to show for it. And it's impossible to tell which calculated risks will pay off and which won't without the benefit of hindsight.

Since we can't live life backwards, doesn't it make sense to make sure we're as protected as possible and set up for financial success in all scenarios, not just the ones that work out according to our hopes? Remember that the question here is *when*, not *if*, you will die. There's no way to say to St. Peter, "No, wait, my investment portfolio hasn't matured yet--can you come back for me in ten years?" Incidentally, this brings up one important part of life insurance we haven't talked about yet: the death benefit. Failed investments don't leave any money behind to take care of your loved ones after you die, but even a whole life policy that's been heavily borrowed against still offers a death benefit.

And third, just because you have a lot of money doesn't mean you'll be good at managing it for long-term reliability. A large percentage of high-achieving people are phenomenal at what they do in their businesses but terrible at managing their own money. Then there's the market...how many people lost huge sums in stocks and real estate in the 2008-2009 financial crisis? The assumption that all successful people know how to manage their finances, or that becoming rich means all your money worries are over, is just plain wrong. Wealth without the right protection won't automatically keep you safe, which is why whole life is so important. It helps people at all financial levels protect themselves.

Besides, net worth isn't exactly great at replacing income. Long-term medical care and other disasters can quickly deplete your assets, often much faster than you can replace them. Your whole life policy, on the other hand, can assist you in many different situations. You won't have to worry about your assets running out because you can turn to your cash value when you need it. If you borrow against it, your gross cash value will remain intact and the rest of the death benefit will be there to replace the spent assets.

And that's not even mentioning the fact that life insurance is about a lot more than having enough money to cover you in an emergency. If all your money is set aside waiting for a disaster or tied up in investments, you won't have a chance to pursue opportunity or enjoyment with it. With a whole life insurance policy, you get the benefit of protection as well as the security and flexibility of your cash value, which will allow you to live life to the fullest.

(If self-insurers buy any life insurance, incidentally, it's usually the cheapest term life policy they can find, so they can devote the rest of their resources to accumulating more assets through investing. This is the essence of the common advice "buy term insurance and invest the difference," which we'll talk more about in section 3 of this book.)

As great as it is to be able to DIY your financial strategy, there are times where even the most savvy people need to bring in expert help and build external support. After all, this isn't a house or a car or even your health we're talking about here. This is your life. It's the most unique, personal, and irreplaceable thing you have. Self-insuring it by betting on the stock market seems like really long odds to us.

Kim D. H. Butler and Jack Burns

Part 2:

AGE, FAMILY, AND TIMING LIES

THE NEXT MORNING...

Stephen finished refilling everyone's coffee and dropped onto the couch next to Kara. She gave him a grateful smile before looking around the room. Next to Kara and Stephen was Kara's oldest sister Elaine, with Victor perched on the sturdy arm of the couch beside her. David, Kara's only brother and next-oldest sibling, occupied the loveseat along with their mother. Three cousins sat in various chairs along the far wall of the den, while a fourth stretched her legs out along the floor with her back against the fireplace hearth. Bill Harding had taken up position in his usual armchair by Kara's end of the couch, a half-finished crossword puzzle on the corner table at his elbow.

"So, those are the reasons why your mother and I chose to pursue life insurance despite all the objections people brought up at dinner yesterday," he said, stirring sugar into his coffee. "And don't think we didn't hear those same arguments that came up at dinner yester-day forty years ago. We sure did, and then some. But we're happy

with the decision we made, and over time we've seen most of those concerns come to nothing. Everyone with me so far?"

There was a round of nods in response. "Alright then," said Grandpa Bill. "What else can we tell you? What other questions or concerns have you run into?"

Elaine rubbed her forehead. "I'm still just processing all of this. I always thought insurance was to pay for the funeral, and maybe give the survivors some money. Nothing like what you're talking about, Dad."

"I heard if you don't start it by your mid-twenties, you may as well not bother," chimed in Lauren, the fireplace cousin, who was a couple years older than Kara. "The older you get, the more expensive and harder to get it will be."

"How do you know your family even needs the coverage?" asked David. "Like, we all work and take care of ourselves, Mom. We'd hate if something happened to you or Dad of course, but we don't necessarily need coverage or money from you if it does."

Stephen cleared his throat and squeezed Kara's hand. They'd decided giving away their secret was worth finding out the information they wanted. "Kara and I are hoping to be expecting soon. What should we do? Insuring ourselves sounds like a good idea, but what about the little one? Should we insure him or her, too?"

"Or the other way around," added Elaine, smiling at her sister. "Vic and I aren't planning on children. Do we even need life insurance at all?"

"Alright, these all sound like questions about age, family, and timing," said Grandma Liza. "Perfect for this gathering!" Everyone laughed.

"So let's start with Elaine and then work our way back around to her. The issue you brought up, E, is that life insurance is often thought of only as death insurance..."

Kara leaned back against her husband and settled in to listen.

Lie #8:
LIFE INSURANCE IS JUST FOR BURIAL COSTS

This lie is a symptom of life insurance being thought of as "death insurance." "Death insurance" really only means a couple of things, and paying for the burial is one of them--not a bad idea, actually, since funerals and burial costs can be quite high. "Death insurance" also means replacing the income the deceased person provided. If a working mom dies, her family needs her income to survive. Or if a stay-at-home dad dies, all the things he does for the kids and the home now have to be done by someone else. And in the rare instance when a death benefit is paid on a child's policy to a parent, "death insurance" allows grieving parents much-needed time off of work to recover from their devastating loss.

So yes, "death insurance" does all of these things. Its job is to protect your Human Life Value (HLV), the amount of financial value your entire life's work represents.

Here's how HLV works in this situation. Let's say you were hit by a drunk driver last night (though we certainly hope that didn't actually happen!). Your family wouldn't sue the driver just for your burial costs. Instead, they would have an attorney figure out the wages you lost by dying before you could earn them, and sue for that amount.

Chances are, you're going to die of a natural cause, not an accident or through someone else's fault. Does your family deserve less based on how you die? Of course not. That's why your life insurance is meant to protect your entire Human Life Value, regardless of how you might die.

Now, if whole life insurance stopped there and didn't do anything else, it really would be "death insurance." But as we've seen throughout the first section of the book, life insurance has many uses while you're still alive.

Remember, when you pay money into a whole life policy, those premium payments build up the cash value we talked about in the last section, not just a far-off death benefit. That cash value is an asset you can either use directly (removing the cash value like a bank withdrawal) or borrow against (leveraging against it like a home equity loan). Borrowing against your cash value is a great option because you're using your money as collateral without actually taking the money out.

Let's say you have a gross cash value of $100,000 and you decide to borrow $40,000 for a down payment on your new home. Your account will continue to grow as if there's still $100,000 in it, while at the same time, you'll have a loan for $40,000 that costs you some interest that you pay to the insurance company for the use of their money. You haven't actually taken anything out of your account. You're borrowing against it, so your loan is actually coming from the company's funds and your cash value is the collateral. This way, your policy will continue to grow at the same rate and your cash value will keep on building.

And whether you borrow or withdraw, there are no limitations on what you can use that money for. You can take that dream vacation and actually relax and enjoy it instead of fretting about how you're affording it all. Perhaps your growing family needs a new home with more space. Maybe that kitchen could finally use some updating.

Busting the Life Insurance Lies

The kids are getting older and will be off to college before you know it. Your cash value can take these things and transform them into opportunities. And every time you pay the loan back (don't forget you'll need to do that!), that money becomes available again for another use.

So when people make the mistake of associating life insurance with death, tragedies, and emergencies, it can be easy to think of it as just something for burial costs. But the real goal of life insurance is to allow you to enjoy your life. The money in your whole life policy is liquid for a reason. It's meant for you to access and use to help you fulfill your dreams and goals. After all, it's *your* money, and you can use it now, not just after someone dies.

Lie #9:
ONLY PEOPLE WITH DEPENDENTS NEED LIFE INSURANCE

This lie is "death insurance" part two. Again, many people believe the only job of a life insurance policy is to provide for your kids after you pass. So if you don't have kids, you don't need life insurance, right?

Wrong. As we're starting to see here, life insurance isn't just "death insurance," it's also a cash-storing and wealth-building asset. Lots of people without kids have assets. Saying childless people don't need life insurance is a bit like saying they don't need a house with more than one bedroom. Technically they don't need the extra rooms because they don't have family members to fill them, yes, but there are a dozen other ways having a larger, roomier house can benefit a single person or couple who can afford to live in one. They can invite guests to stay with them, convert a bedroom into an office or a home gym, rent the extra room(s) out on Airbnb for cash or get roommates to save cash, use the house as collateral for a loan, etc.

Life insurance works similarly. Maybe you don't have kids to identify as beneficiaries, but you can use the asset of your policy's cash value to pursue a dozen other opportunities over the course of your life.

Here's one example: in 2006, a woman we know went through a divorce, left her full-time job, and started a coaching business. She was 35 years old, had two young sons, and no steady income. She was basically starting over from zero. Now, in most cases like this, what happens? The woman either goes through a really lean time until she starts to succeed, or she goes through a really lean time until she quits and gets another day job. And while we all love warm fuzzy "you're gonna make it after all!" success stories, the sad truth is that most people fall into the second category.

Not this woman. About fifteen years earlier, well before she got married and had her sons, she started a whole life insurance policy. It wasn't a big policy--she only paid $100/month at the very beginning. But over those fifteen years, her cash value had built up enough that she could borrow against it for quite a bit. So she did just that--and funded the first two years of her business, not to mention living expenses for herself and her kids, all from that one policy! She's since paid her policy loans back in full, her business now supports her and her family full time, and both her sons have their own whole life policies.

This is a great story for many reasons, but most important with regards to this lie is that this woman didn't have kids when she started the policy! She knew she wanted them eventually, but she also knew that she had time, and decided to use that time to start building up cash value for herself. That decision later allowed her to support the kids she didn't yet have when she started. So you don't have to wait until you have a bundle of joy on the way to start thinking about your future finances and insurance.

And this works even if you never intend to have children, or even if you have no family at all. One of our clients in Chicago works for a church that does significant charitable work in its area. This man is single, has no siblings, and his parents have passed on, so he chose to list the church's charity as his beneficiary. While we will help him use the cash value in such a way to minimize his death benefit, there will be some left over (which there must be, so he isn't taxed on any of the loans that may be outstanding at time of death) which will go to this church's charity. He was very pleased with this arrangement, as he sees the value of the living benefit while alive and the chance to leave a small lump sum to his charity upon death.

Incidentally, some time after making this arrangement, this man was asked to serve on the charity's board of trustees. Whether or not you have children, whole life insurance gives you an opportunity to leave the legacy you want to leave, which helps you live the life you want to live now.

Also, many people are waiting longer to start families these days, and there are some incredible benefits to starting a life insurance policy while you're young, whether you have children or not. Younger people are often healthier, which means you are a much lower risk for insurance companies to cover. This means lower premiums, which means saving money. And with a whole life policy, your premiums will never go up based on changes in your health. So if you develop health issues at fifty that you didn't have when you were thirty, you'd still pay the same amount...*if* you started the policy at thirty. Trying to start it at fifty, now that you're both older and in poorer health, will be more expensive. Your family, if you have one, may have to bear the burden of that extra cost.

And finally, when you get a whole life insurance policy in your 20s or 30s, your cash value will have literally decades to grow. The nature of whole life insurance is just that: it's there for your whole life, building up cash value. As we mentioned above, that cash value can be a key to whether you can support your children's education or enjoy independence in your later years, or you instead have to rely on your children to support you once you reach your 70s and 80s.

So whether you have kids now, you want them soon, or you never want them, you can still consider a whole life policy. Its benefits can work for you no matter your family situation.

Lie #10:
NEVER BUY LIFE INSURANCE FOR A CHILD

It's an interesting phenomenon that while many people believe that you need to have kids to need life insurance, you should never insure the kids themselves. This is another "death insurance" lie--since kids have no income, insuring them is supposedly a waste of money.

But that mindset is part of the myth we'd like to bust here. Insuring your child has very little to do with their future earning capacity, or with a death benefit. Insuring your child is about building wealth... first for you, and then, for them. This wealth will grow for years and even generations to come. It's actually a very solid financial strategy, for several reasons.

Remember how the younger you are, the easier you are to insure? And the higher that policy's internal rate of return is? Imagine how low the premiums will be to insure a healthy child. While lower premiums equate to a lower cash value, the rate of return on that cash value is higher. Then, with a whole life policy, those premiums will stay the same for the child's whole life, regardless of their future health. Many whole life policies also offer the option to purchase additional insurance regardless of future insurability. In other words, since they will already be insured, any future health problems that they may have won't prevent them from getting additional insurance they may want in later years.

On the other hand, there can be a lot of value in insuring a grown child as well. If you're 65 and your child is 40, insuring them (instead of grandchildren) will build a lot more cash value since there's higher premium availability in adulthood than in childhood. And the cash value's internal rate of return on a policy insuring your 40 year old child will typically be higher than if you purchased the insurance on yourself at age 65.

Remember, the cash value component of a whole life policy functions as a savings component. As the policy *owner*, your savings in the policy you own on your adult child or grandchild is cash value that is liquid and flexible. Unlike many other types of savings vehicles, your money isn't tied up or controlled by other entities who decide how and when you can access the funds. Since you are the policy *owner*, you have access to the cash whenever you want through withdrawals or policy loans. You can help your adult children with it if you want, or use it for your grandchildren, all with the help of the cash value that has been building in that whole life policy.

And keep in mind – because it's *your* policy and your money, you can also use that cash value for yourself, if needed. You may intend to use the money for your child, but wouldn't it be valuable to have the option to borrow against or withdraw the cash value "just in case"? One of the greatest gifts you can give your children is to remain self-sufficient, and whole life insurance helps you do that, as well as ensure that your loved ones will receive an additional death benefit someday.

Plus, a whole life policy is a tax-advantaged account, so the savings in it will grow tax-deferred.

And since the rate of return in whole life policies is around 3.5%-5% (as of this writing in 2016), you'll be getting a much higher rate of return than you would saving in CDs, savings accounts, money market funds or fixed deferred annuities. The average rate of return on whole life cash value is almost always 2 or 3 percentage points above bank savings accounts rates and money market accounts.

Just imagine the serious cash value you'd be building if every parent and child in your family had a whole life policy. (Heck, imagine if your parents had gotten a whole life policy for you!) We call this "family banking," and it's a powerful inter-generational wealth-building strategy that enables families to accomplish more together than they could alone, providing financing for first cars, home down payments, education funds, business start up costs, and more.

And as if all that weren't enough, insuring a child also provides you with some pretty special estate planning benefits. Life insurance is the absolute best way to transfer your wealth to your heirs. Why? Because by transferring a policy you own to the insured child or children, the money you pass down through the policy transfer is not subject to income taxes. And if the cash value is larger than what you could gift annually (currently $14,000), you can always start to purposely use up your lifetime exemption. You'll be required to fill out IRS form 709 to report the gift, but no taxes will be due. (Currently, federal estate tax only applies to heirs but not spouses on estates over $5.45 million, or $10.9 million for couples, when properly set up.)

So insuring your children is by no means a waste of money. It's a financial strategy that builds wealth over decades and even centuries. The idea is often implemented with a skip in generations, meaning grandparents buy life insurance on grandchildren, each generation repeating the strategy. This may be more than you and your family are ready to do right now, but insuring your children and grandchildren is a proven strategy for generational wealth that is definitely worth exploring when you're ready.

Lie #11:
LIFE INSURANCE ISN'T WORTH IT AFTER A CERTAIN AGE

This lie takes a lot of different forms. Two of the ones we see the most are: "if you don't start young, it's too late" and "you don't need insurance once you're older." And while neither of these are accurate, there are some some valid concerns when it comes to purchasing life insurance later in life. Perhaps you're not in the best of health, you don't think you'd be able to build any value, you have no dependents, or you are on a limited income. All of these are reasons that life insurance after a certain age might not be the best choice for you. But your age itself is rarely the limiting factor in that decision that many people think it is.

The issue behind this lie is that people confuse age with personal situations. If you are over 85, if you have an illness that could be terminal, or if you've had serious medical conditions for 30+ years... then yes, getting life insurance will be difficult for you. But if you're in relatively good health (or in recovery/remission) and you are concerned that it's too late to get insurance because you're 60 or even 70, think again. It may require a higher premium, but it's definitely possible, and it's definitely not too late. (Even if you aren't insurable, there may be a possibility of owning a policy on a child or a grandchildren, so that can be worth exploring at this age as well.)

There are pros and cons to starting a life insurance policy when you're older. The biggest benefit, frankly, is that you get all of the benefits of a life insurance policy we've been talking about so far: a tax-free death benefit, tax-deferred cash value growth, the asset of cash value to borrow against, etc. You can also use your policy to help with things that may be more important later in life, like helping your grandchild through college, starting a travel fund to visit the places you'll finally have time to visit, setting up a reverse mortgage on your home to remove your mortgage payment or even use your equity for income, while still leaving an asset for your heirs, or compensating your adult children for taking care of you or your home.

Also, after a certain age (either 100 or 121, depending on when you bought the policy), whole life policies endow. Endowment means that the cash value and the death benefit value are now equal, and upon reaching endowment, your policy pays you its entire cash value. (For an illustration of endowment, see Appendix D.) Not everyone will live to see this happen, but more and more people are living longer and longer these days. It's well within the realm of possibility that you'd live to see a policy endow even if you bought it at 60 or 70.

The major issue that comes up around starting a life insurance policy later in life is that it won't really start helping you financially right away. In fact, for the first few years (while its cash value starts to build up) it will cost you more money than you'll be able to get out of it. This is where the lie of "if you don't start young, it's too late" mostly comes from--when you're 20 or 30, paying premiums for quite a few years to get a future benefit is relatively easy. At 60 or 70, it can be harder. Especially if you don't have a lot of income to begin with, as many of today's retirees sadly don't.

This is why your personal situation is so important to this decision. If you are 70 and in poor health, on a fixed income, without heirs, and/or with a family history of dying by 75, life insurance probably isn't right for you. But if you're 70 and healthy, you have some extra income, you have a family to leave a death benefit to, and/or you anticipate living another 20+ years, life insurance might be a great option for you. Furthermore, if you have a large estate, life insurance can enable you to implement more efficient strategies in estate planning than families with no life insurance.

Since this is a complex but very important concept that we could write its own section about if we had the space, we invite you to download a free 16-page special report and video presentation at ProsperityPeaks.com/permission. This report, called "Permission To Spend," specifically addresses how life insurance can be used to lower income taxes and draw down other assets in a way that increases cash flow (without wasting dollars) once you're over 70.

If you'd like to get life insurance and you're older, don't just assume that you can't or that it won't help you. Talk to an advisor who specializes in working with elderly policy owners. They'll be able to tell you the right answer for your unique situation.

Lie #12:
MY FAMILY DOESN'T NEED LIFE INSURANCE

There are a lot of different reasons this one comes up. People say things like:

- My spouse works, so even if I die, we're okay.

- My kids will be grown by the time I die, so insurance isn't necessary.

- My family doesn't need a lot of money.

- I don't want to make my spouse rich.

And all of those things might be true. But remember, life insurance is much more than just replacement income. Each of these reasons only looks at it through that narrow lens.

So first of all, if you are only looking at life insurance as replacement income, it's almost impossible to predict what level of income you'll need to replace in ten or twenty or fifty years. You can run calculations for days and still not truly figure out what your financial "needs" will be that far out. And obviously, you have no idea when you'll actually die. By these arguments alone, it's pretty clear that life insurance is still a pretty good idea--and that guessing how much you need or when you'll need it doesn't work very well.

Instead, consider your own Human Life Value. Your HLV is the value of all your future earnings. So if you make $50,000 per year and you anticipate you'll make that same amount for the next thirty years, your HLV is $1.5 million. (If you're a stay-at-home parent or a volunteer, you can estimate your HLV by assigning an hourly or yearly value to the work you do.) Your life insurance policy needs to replace that *future* income--or the work you do to earn it--so that if you did die tomorrow and your family earned no other money ever, they'd still be taken care of.

It may also help here to separate life insurance from the idea of needs and focus it more on desires. For instance, the average American family spends 35% of its income servicing debt. No one *needs* to do anything differently with that money, but if you're spending a third of what you bring in on something that never gives you anything back, wouldn't you want to change that? So the question isn't necessarily whether you need life insurance (or a 401(k) or IRA or other savings or investment vehicle), the question is how to start trimming that 35% down so you can keep more of your own money.

For our money, whole life is the best way to start doing that, as it allows you to become your own financial institution rather than relying on external ones. Recall that when you are your own bank, so to speak, you don't have to qualify to borrow money, repay on a schedule someone else sets, take a hit to your credit score if you miss a payment, pay double-digit interest rates or management fees, etc. You still have to manage your cash flow, pay your premiums, and pay back what you borrow against your policy's cash value, but at the end of the day all of that money is yours (except the interest paid to the insurance company), not a bank's or a broker's. And in that light, it makes sense to have as much life insurance as you can afford.

For those of you who don't want to make your spouses rich...we're not entirely sure where this objection comes from. If you're in a happy marriage or partnership, you and your partner will likely be happy to both have policies, so each is taken care of if the other passes first. If your partnership isn't a happy one, you can always change the beneficiary of your policy, so there's little reason for concern there, either.

Plus, life insurance isn't designed to make anyone rich. It's designed to replace income, income from work, or income from assets, in our later years. No company would issue insurance for a higher amount than you'd earn during your working lifetime, or for more than the potential value of your estate. So unless you're already rich, your insurance won't make your spouse rich after you die.

***

Kara stretched as she rose from the couch. The insurance meeting was breaking up now, with David and two cousins starting to talk football again, Elaine and Victor asking Grandma Liza about the latest cruise she and Grandpa Bill had taken, and the rest scattering to find leftovers to munch on.

"How are you feeling about all this now, K?" asked Bill Harding as he retrieved his crossword.

"Mmmm, much better, Dad," she replied.

"Right, it doesn't seem nearly as much like a foreign language now!" said Stephen with a wink.

"Glad to hear it. I'm betting you'll run into more questions once you start looking around, though. Don't hesitate to call us when you do- -unless we're on some godforsaken boat somewhere, we'll be here to help."

Kara grinned. It was a running joke between her parents that while Bill did in fact enjoy the frequent cruises, he often pretended not to until he actually got on board.

"No problem, Dad. We'll definitely let you know."

Part 3:

TERM VS.
WHOLE LIFE LIES

In this section, Kara and Stephen run across the biggest argument in life insurance. Fortunately, they've got Grandpa Bill to help them out.

Four months later...

"Hello, Harding residence!" Bill's voice was its usual hearty self over the phone.

"Hi Dad, it's Kara," she said.

"And me!" Stephen called from across the room. Kara rolled her eyes and grinned as she put the phone on speaker.

"Well, good morning to you both!" Bill rumbled. "Liza's at the store, so I'm holding down the fort today. What can I do for you?"

"Well, we've got good news. We're finally expecting!"

"That's wonderful! I'll have your mother call as soon as she gets back. How far along are you now, K?"

"A little less than two months. We were pretty sure a couple weeks ago, and Dr. Harper confirmed it this morning."

"Fantastic. I'm so happy for you two. I know you've been waiting for this. Well, shall I get off the line so you can call your sisters? Jeanne will moan about you not calling her the very minute you found out, but you probably ought to tell her anyway."

Kara laughed. "Oh, I know she will. But Jeanne can wait a bit longer. We actually wanted to ask you something else first."

"Of course, kids. What do you need?"

Stephen slid onto the kitchen bench behind his wife, slipping his arms gently around her waist. "Remember at Thanksgiving when we talked about life insurance?" he asked.

"Certainly. Did you come up with more questions?"

"Oh, did we ever," Stephen groaned. Kara stifled a giggle. "What's the deal with this term insurance versus whole life insurance thing? Everyone I talk to has something different to say about it, and some people get REALLY upset! It's like the Jets and the Sharks over here, and I don't know which side's going to start dance-fighting first."

Kara gave up trying to contain her laughter. Say what you want about marrying a former amateur actor, *she thought,* it's never boring!

Bill was laughing, too. "Stay cool, boy," he cracked, quoting the same musical Stephen had referenced. "It's not nearly as bad as it sounds."

"We know that you and Mom got the whole life thing you were telling us about," Kara said. "But Stephen's right. We're running into a lot of people who say to go with term instead. Even some experts on TV are talking about it!"

"And I've run some numbers," Stephen continued. "The premiums on term insurance are a lot cheaper than whole life. We're not hurt-

ing for cash exactly, but I certainly wouldn't mind saving some now that Junior's coming."

"Ah, yes. I know exactly how you feel," said Bill. "This was a big question Liza and I ran into as well--I think we'd have talked about it at Thanksgiving if we'd had more time. Let me tell you what our insurance advisor told me about it."

Kara pulled a legal pad and pen toward her as Bill began relating this new information.

Lie #13:
FINANCIAL EXPERTS RECOMMEND AGAINST WHOLE LIFE

This lie right here is one of the main reasons this book exists. As Stephen and Kara discovered, term vs. whole life is the loudest argument in the life insurance industry, and one reason that argument persists is that a lot of so-called financial experts have come out in favor of term--and trashed whole life--from their soapboxes and spotlights on TV.

Because TV presence implies credibility, people assume that because these "experts" are on TV, they must be giving quality advice. And most of them have made fortunes for themselves, so it seems to make sense that they'd know a thing or two about money, investing, and various financial products. But the sad truth is that most of these big names are giving financial advice without actually having any qualifications to do so. Many of them don't even follow the advice they give on TV, telling their audiences one thing but doing something else behind closed doors.

One of the most well-known financial "experts" is a great example of someone who doesn't follow her own advice. (We're not naming names in this book, but you can probably figure out who we mean... or find several others like her.) She routinely recommends investing in the stock market, for example. But does she do this herself? Nope. She puts her own money in relatively safe municipal bonds. This "expert" also recommends against permanent life insurance, including whole life, when a few years back, she used to swear by whole life policies. At some point along the way, she decided to change her tune and has been tearing down permanent life insurance ever since. So which is it? Do you believe what she used to say, or what she's saying now?

The point is: don't believe everything that the people with publicity say simply because they are on TV or in a magazine. Remember that the number one goal of people in the spotlight is to stay there. One way they do this is through creating controversy, and another way is by keeping their advertisers (often large financial corporations that sell term insurance and/or mutual funds) happy. They don't want to hurt you, but helping you find the right insurance policy for your individual situation is not their job or concern. So don't just pay attention to what they say; pay attention to what they do. If a well-known expert tells you to invest one way but invests their own money somewhere else, or advises their personal clients differently, that's a huge red flag.

There are many life insurance advisors out there who do understand the benefits of whole life, and want their clients to experience those benefits if the situation is right for them. Most advisors know that whole life has been around for centuries for a reason, because it is truly a sound financial product.

So if you want the truth (and the best option for your individual situation), the best thing you can do is to find an experienced life insurance advisor who has seen the benefits of whole life in their clients' lives, and listen to them over a celebrity with a TV show.

Busting the Life Insurance Lies

Lie #14:
WHOLE LIFE OR TERM LIFE? YOU HAVE TO PICK ONE OR THE OTHER!

This is a special kind of lie called a false dichotomy or false dilemma. A false dichotomy (pronounced "dye-COT-uh-mee") is a situation where someone presents two options as if they are the only two options available, in the hope that you'll choose their side over the other.

A classic example is "if you're not with us, you're against us." There are actually at least three other options in that situation (you could dislike both sides and prefer a third choice, sympathize with both sides in some way, or be totally indifferent), but the person who makes that statement is creating a false dichotomy to try and force you to make a decision.

False dichotomies also completely disregard the option of having both choices. In 2014, the Ford motor company ran an ad campaign for its new Fusion Hybrid called "And Is Better" that illustrated this perfectly. These ads took common phrases and highlighted how terrible they would be if the word "and" was replaced with "or."

Think about their examples:

Nuts *or* bolts?

Sweet *or* sour?

Large *or* in charge?

Aside from being hilarious and memorable, these ads proved their point—getting both options is not only possible, but is way better than choosing one or the other.

Term life vs. whole life has become a classic false dichotomy in the insurance industry. Not only are both valuable in their own ways, but you don't actually have to choose between them. We're *writing this book* to sing the praises of whole life insurance, but *even we* recognize that term life can be valuable (or even essential, to reach your full Human Life Value) sometimes. And there are ways to use both term life and whole life to your advantage, rather than having to choose one or the other.

Term life insurance, often shortened to just "term," means exactly what it says: a temporary insurance that lasts for a "term" of several years and will have to be renewed or cancelled at the end of that term. Many people go with term because it appears cheaper at first (lower premiums, clear expiration date). Whole life is just as we've described it so far, insurance meant to build cash value for your whole life. See, the question of term or whole life is really a question of "now or later." And like the famous candy, you really can have both.

As we mentioned in lie #2, if premiums are a challenge for you in your present situation, combining term and permanent may actually be a great solution for you. You can start out with term if you need inexpensive coverage right away, and then transition into a permanent policy like whole life. This ensures that all the money you pay into your term policy doesn't just disappear, as it would if you only kept the term insurance. And once you convert all or a portion of your term policy to a whole life policy, you won't have to worry about your premiums going up any further.

Having a mixture of term and whole life can be a great way to fund

Busting the Life Insurance Lies

your entire Human Life Value. If you want to get the appropriate policy but 100% whole life is not within your financial reach at the moment, starting out with a term policy (or a combination of both) is a good place to start until you do have the means to fund a (or an additional) whole life policy. You may also want to consider getting a term policy while you wait for your whole life policy approval, which can take weeks or even months to kick in.

When it comes to life insurance, it's not just a "one or the other" deal. You can have both term and permanent or whole life insurance, and many people benefit from having both types of policies in play. It's all up to your situation and what will suit your capability now and going forward into the future. Don't let anyone use a false dichotomy to pressure you into choosing one or the other. "Both" just might be the best answer for your situation. (See Appendices B4 and B5.)

Lie #15:
"BUY TERM AND INVEST THE DIFFERENCE" WORKS

Having said that term insurance can play a valuable role in some people's financial picture, there is some advice out there regarding term insurance that just doesn't work. This is one example--probably the biggest one.

"Buy term and invest the difference" is a classic piece of financial advice that almost everyone has heard at some point or other. What this phrase means is that you should pay a cheaper premium for term insurance and invest the leftover money--the difference between the term premium and a whole life premium--elsewhere. It sounds like a good idea in theory, but it comes with some serious pitfalls that you don't want to get caught in.

The big question here is: where do you invest that leftover cash? A lot of people turn to 401(k)s, mutual funds, or IRAs. Yet, as we've seen, none of those give you any freedom with your own money! With 401(k)s, for example, you can't touch the money inside the account until you reach a certain age. What if an emergency or an amazing opportunity comes up and you need access to the money now? Either you can't get to it, or you have to pay a stiff early access penalty, plus taxes to the IRS, which completely defeats the purpose of having the extra money in the first place. And if you invest *outside* of a 401(k), IRA, or other qualified retirement plan, your investment

Busting the Life Insurance Lies

will be subjected to taxes every year, taxes that will drain the value of your investment and lower your rate of return.

The other problem with this lie is that, as we discussed earlier, these investment accounts aren't actually savings vehicles, they're typically stock market investments. You don't have ready access to the money in them--and that money is always at risk. The stock market is always changing, which means so is the value of your investment accounts. When the time comes for you to redeem your shares and access your money, you may find that they are worth far less than when you started. Recall how millions of people discovered they were in that exact situation during the stock market collapse of 2008. Many who had to make withdrawals or sell homes during that time ended up with nothing and had to start over from square one (or, as some called it, ground zero).

On the other hand, a whole life policy *is* in fact a savings vehicle. The cash value component of whole life allows you to put your premium into a safe policy that is saved for you to use later by withdrawing it or borrowing against it. It takes a few years to build up the cash value in a whole life policy, but it has no penalties, no withdrawal fees, no waiting period to access the value once it's built up, and no risk of losing that value in a volatile stock market. This is why we see it as the best option out there for storing cash.

While term life insurance can provide immediate and inexpensive coverage, it isn't a savings vehicle either. Any money you put into a term policy vanishes for good when the policy expires--which is actually what you want with a term policy, because if the policy expires, that means you haven't expired yourself! (And you can often convert term insurance to whole life as it expires, too.)

So if all you need is cheap, immediate coverage, buying term is a good temporary solution, but if you want to build value long-term, investing the difference is only minimally beneficial. A whole life policy is a much stronger option. (See Appendix G.)

Which brings us to...

Lie #16:
WHOLE LIFE INSURANCE IS TOO EXPENSIVE AND TERM'S PRICE IS RIGHT

This lie has a grain of truth in it, at least at first. Cheap term premiums are attractive, and many people don't give it much thought beyond that. But the kicker comes when it's time to renew your policy. Renewing a term policy nearly always results in much higher premiums...and you may not hear a thing about that rate hike until you look at your policy upon renewal. Suddenly you're faced with a much bigger expense that you didn't know you needed to budget for.

Oops.

With whole life, what you see is what you get. You may be nervous about that higher premium now (and as we discussed earlier, starting with term and changing over to permanent whole life is an option here), but that premium will remain constant for the entire life of the policy. You will always know exactly what you need to pay and you can build that into your budget literally for the rest of your life. And the premium doesn't have to be paid for your entire life either, just as long as possible to build optimal value.

The same can't be said for term. Your premiums will go up, and over time they will get bigger than whole life premiums. Plus, if your term insurance expires while you're still alive, as it does for 99% of policyholders (fortunately for them), all the money that you pour into your term policy disappears for good. That won't happen with permanent whole life insurance. Any money you put in will build your cash value forever.

Perhaps the closest parallel here is between renting and buying a home. Renting appears cheaper at first, it has some perks that buying doesn't (like having a landlord who takes care of repairs for you), and it allows less-established people to afford a place to live. But over time, rents increase...and increase...and increase again. Eventually, your rent will be higher than a mortgage would be (if it didn't start there, which it sometimes does), and you'll have no equity. Sometimes people are forced to move out of neighborhoods they've lived in for years if they can't afford the rent anymore.

Buying often seems pricier up front, so the barrier to entry may be a bit higher, but as a buyer, you can lock in a fixed mortgage rate that's guaranteed for the life of the loan. By the time the house is paid off, what started out as a high payment will likely feel ridiculously low--just ask your parents or grandparents who bought houses in the 1950s, 1960s, and 1970s (and likely sold them years later for ten or twenty times what they paid). As long as you're current with those payments, you can never be forced out of a house. And since you're building equity in the house, you can use it as a collateral asset for yourself.

A whole life policy works exactly the same way. You're purchasing an asset, not "renting" a policy temporarily. But unlike a home, you'll never have to fix a water heater, mow the lawn, or replace the roof!

Also, remember that some whole life policies actually pay you back! Remember how we touched on mutual companies in an earlier section? Those companies treat policyholders as owners of the company, because they are. All of the company's profits go back to you, the policyholder, as dividends. Yes, you! You can use that dividend

Busting the Life Insurance Lies

in many ways. It could go toward your premium or building your cash value or you can cash the dividend check and use it how you want. That's a great bonus that you definitely will not get from a term policy.

The bottom line is that term policies start off cheap and then ramp up, first slowly and then with a vengeance, until they become out of reach for almost anyone. It's very common to save money up front, but then to realize, as your policy nears the end of its term, that you'll have to pay a LOT more if you want a new policy. In our rent vs. buy analogy, it's as if your landlord suddenly hikes up your rent so high, you can't even imagine paying that much! We think you deserve to know exactly what you're getting into when you commit to something as important as a life insurance policy. You may be a little intimidated by the premiums that come with whole life policies, but the cash value growth and the possibility for dividends more than make up for it.

Lie #17:
THE INSURANCE COMPANY KEEPS YOUR WHOLE LIFE CASH VALUE WHEN YOU DIE

This is really a misunderstanding of what "cash value" actually is. What this lie is really saying is hey, when I die, the insurance company keeps all the money I've saved! While this is clearly not accurate (if it were, there would be no point in building your cash value at all), there's a lot of confusion around how whole life works, and very little clarity around what happens to the money you pay into your policy.

This lie fits into the term vs. whole life category because it ascribes to whole life something that actually happens with term. When a term policy expires, neither you nor your beneficiary gets anything from it. The death benefit vanishes, and all the money you paid in as premiums disappears forever into the coffers of the insurance company. As noted previously, this is one of the biggest drawbacks of buying term and never converting it to whole life.

When a whole life policy expires--that is, when *you* expire--things happen differently. With whole life, your very first premium payment puts a permanent death benefit in place. Not just a 1% chance of a death benefit, but a 100% chance of a death benefit, as long as you keep the policy in force.

Unlike with term insurance, the company takes a huge risk guaranteeing the death benefit up front with whole life. If you take out a policy on yourself today and accidentally walk in front a bus tomorrow (please don't!), the company is on the hook for your entire death benefit, even though you'd only paid them a small fraction of that amount up front. And even if the company doesn't have to pay your death benefit for many years, it will have to pay it eventually because you will eventually die. This is not like term, where the company gambles that most of its clients will survive their policies and makes a profit by not having to pay many death benefits.

But all of this is about the death benefit. How does cash value play into this equation? And if the insurance company doesn't keep your cash value, what does happen to it?

To understand how cash value works, let's look at the lifespan of a whole life policy. If you've ever played the original version of Monopoly, the classic board game, you may have discovered a helpful clue. One of the cards a player can draw from the "Community Chest" pile says, "Life insurance matures – Collect $100!" The player happily accepts a $100 Monopoly bill (the game was created about 100 years ago, so you'd likely be adding add some zeroes to that number now), but what does it really mean?

When a policy matures, or endows, the cash value *equals* the death benefit, and the policyholder can receive--or be "endowed" with-- the full death benefit. Yes, even if they are still alive! And the death benefit at endowment isn't the same death benefit you started with. It's typically many times larger than the original policy death benefit. As a rule of thumb, the younger you were when the policy started and the longer you've held it since then, the larger it will grow.

Cash value grows, too, slowly at first, but very steadily. The premiums fund the cash value while also continually *increasing* the death benefit. Both the death benefit and the cash value keep growing, until the cash value eventually "catches up" to the death benefit at endowment. In this way, the growing cash account builds value for and benefits both the company and the policyholder. We are used to company vs. client battles, but remember that with a mutual company, the policyholders are the company, so a policy must be "win-win."

The vast majority of policyholders will pass on years bears before their policies endow. And when that happens, the beneficiaries will receive the full death benefit (minus any policy loans), which has grown over time and which includes the cash value. Cash value is not a separate part of the policy (savings to the left, death benefit to the right), as this lie suggests; it's more correctly understood as *the part of the policy the policyholder has access to.*

Remember, cash value is the portion of your life insurance policy that you can borrow against and use as collateral. Or, if you prefer, it's the part of the policy you can simply withdraw and keep. It's the part of the policy you can USE as "yours," because it is yours!

Another way to understand it could be equating your cash value to the equity in your home, which you build gradually as you make mortgage payments. The death benefit is comparable to the total value of the home. When you pay off your mortgage, your equity and the home's value are one and the same. And when a policy endows, the policy's full value (the death benefit) and the policy's equity (the cash value) are also one and the same. (See Appendix D.)

You might buy a home for $250k that will be worth $1 million years later when the mortgage is paid off. If you sell the home before the mortgage is paid off, perhaps the home is now worth $600k and your mortgage is paid down to $150k, so you'll keep the difference, or $450k.

A whole life policy works similarly, except the death benefit is guaranteed to keep increasing as long as premiums are paid and cash value increases, which is not the case with the housing market! You're buying a sizable asset (literally, a policy is an asset you can even re-sell, in some cases), and you're building equity with every payment you make. The cash value is the equity you can use, and the death benefit represents the total value of the asset. So your beneficiaries receive the entire net death benefit, which *includes* the cash value you have built in the policy.

If you withdraw cash value, your death benefit decreases accordingly, because you have reduced the "equity" of your policy. If you have outstanding loans against your cash value, these will be subtracted from the death benefit, just like if you have a HELOC (Home Equity Line of Credit) you'll have to repay the bank the withdrawn portion of the line of credit if you sell your home. This isn't "unfair," it actually makes perfect sense that the more equity you have in any asset, the more it is worth.

The biggest difference between how home equity works and how cash value works is that when you make your first home payment, you have *no* equity (other than your down payment) and you have to wait years to build value. But with a life insurance policy, you have value immediately. Your net worth increases and your loved ones are protected the moment you make your first premium payment. And as your cash value grows, the value of your policy's death benefit grows, too.

Let's look at an example. The numbers here were copied directly from one of the policy examples in this book's Appendix B1, for a 35-year-old male policy owner with a $100,000 policy.

Policy Year	Owner Age	Net Cash Value	Net Death Benefit
1	35	$0	$100,000
5	39	$10,996	$124,262
10	44	$25,698	$147,987
20	54	$66,065	$197,669
36	70	$173,811	$288,678
41	75	$218,754	$319,819
46	80	$271,300	$356,907
51	85	$331,119	$401,596
56	90	$395,537	$452,205
61	95	$462.524	$501,963
66	100	$557,936	$557,936
76	110	$912,526	$912,526
86	120	$1,492,871	$1,492,871

Notice how as the cash value grows, so does the death benefit. The latter is a direct result of the former. The policy started out at $0 CV and a $100,000 DB. By year 20, the DB had grown to over $197,000, while the CV had grown to just over $66,000.

The death benefit always grows with the cash value, and as you build more cash value, your death benefit is guaranteed to rise. The longer the policy is in force, the more your cash value grows.

In this example, you can see that after 41 years, the death benefit of the policy has grown to over three times the original face value of $100,000, and the cash value, the part you can access or borrow against now, is growing steadily. And if you should die in that 41st year of the policy, the death benefit is awarded tax-free to your heirs in full--the only thing that can reduce it is if you have outstanding policy loans, which the DB pays back first automatically. Meanwhile, if you live to age 100, the cash value catches up to the death benefit. After that, they grow equally until full endowment at age 120.

The insurance company isn't "keeping your cash value" any more than a mortgage company is "keeping your equity" if you sell a home and the existing mortgage is subtracted from your proceeds. You are simply still in the process of building your full use, or equity, in the policy. Your beneficiaries receive the full face value or death benefit from day one, and your death benefit grows over time. Your cash value starts out low and also builds over time until one day, if you lived long enough, it will actually catch up to the growing death benefit and equal the value of the death benefit.

***

"Does that all make more sense now? Clear as mud?" asked Bill.

Kara looked up from her several pages of notes. "I think so, Dad. You've made it pretty clear why you and Mom decided against term insurance in the long run."

"Yeah, I feel much more confident now," added Stephen. "But I gotta tell you, Bill, even knowing this more clearly, I'm still not sure who we should talk to about actually setting it up, how to pay for it, that kind of thing. I know it's been quite a while since you set up your policy...is the advisor you used even still working?"

"Oh no, he retired years ago. But he left me a card of someone to go to if we ever needed anything...hold the line, I'll go dig for it."

A few minutes later, Bill returned with the contact information for an advisor's office in their city. A few minutes after that, Kara had set up an appointment for the following week. Finally she and Stephen felt ready to move forward.

Busting the Life Insurance Lies

Kim D. H. Butler and Jack Burns

Part 4:

PAYMENT AND MONEY LIES

You may have noticed that we haven't talked much about one particular area yet: payment and money. But don't worry! That's what this next part is all about. We know that there are lots of questions (and lies!) around how insurance payments work, what happens if you have to miss a payment, and more. So let's follow Kara and Stephen to their first appointment, where some of those lies will rear their ugly heads.

***

The insurance advisor's office looked like almost any other office building. As Kara got out of the car, she felt a momentary fear that it would be as faceless and impersonal as a tax attorney's office she once temped in. She took Stephen's hand and squeezed it for reassurance.

"It's gonna be fine, hon," he murmured. "They sounded friendly on the phone, right?"

"True enough," she replied. "Okay, let's do this."

The couple were pleasantly surprised to find the office spacious and well-decorated. Someone had obviously taken great care to take a cookie-cutter building and make it as welcoming as possible.

"Good morning!" a smiling receptionist greeted them. "You're the Michaelsons?"

"Last time we checked," cracked Stephen, trusting his usual humor to help put Kara at ease.

"Great. Evan will be ready for you in just a minute."

As the receptionist was speaking, a slim, sandy-haired man in a gray suit came out of the hallway behind her. "You rang?" he joked, then shook hands with both Stephen and Kara and introduced himself as Evan Holmes, the advisor they'd come to meet with.

Over the next half hour, Kara found her nervousness draining away. Evan was attentive and sharp, answering many of their questions with similar information that Grandpa Bill had given them. He also hit it off with Stephen right away, as the two men proved to have similar senses of humor and were soon inserting puns and witticisms into the discussion so quickly that Kara had to laugh. Before she knew it, Evan had gotten a clear picture of their personal financial economy as well as how much money they felt they could comfortably commit to saving each month. He recommended a whole life policy for each of them and one for the baby, in addition to a term policy on each of them for additional coverage, to be converted once the whole life policies were approved. The policy package he described not only gave them great coverage, but also cost less than she'd been afraid it would.

He explained that the combination of the whole life and the term enabled them to start with a monthly savings commitment that they could stick with while still insuring their Human Life Value, which based on their young ages he estimated to be about 25 times their income. He also explained an extra rider their whole life policy had called a Paid-Up Additions (PUA) rider.

"The PUA rider lets you put in more cash monthly or annually to boost the policy's cash value even further," Evan said. "What I typically recommend is for people to maximize their PUAs as soon as possible, since that helps build cash value sooner than premium payments alone, getting you to the break-even point much faster. If you need to borrow against the policy in the first few years, this extra cash value gives you more borrowing power. Plus, with this rider the policy can grow with you--as your capacity to save increases, your cash value can increase with it. Make sense?"

"Yes, I think so," said Stephen. "It sounds like it could be very helpful in a few more years."

"Exactly," said Evan. "Okay, now that was me talking for quite a while. What questions do you two have?"

"I think we have a few questions about payment in general," Kara said. "Can you tell us more about how the premiums work?"

"And what happens if, God forbid, we have to miss one?" Stephen interjected. Kara knew this was a deep-seated fear her husband had after growing up in a household that occasionally had its electricity and water turned off. Even now that they both made and managed their money well, the idea of missing a payment on anything was a huge deal for him.

"Right, and, um..." Kara looked at her notes. "You talked about borrowing, but there are other ways to access our cash value, right?"

Evan nodded reassuringly. "Of course. Let's start with premiums. Your base premiums on the whole life policies are required either monthly or annually, and you can change back and forth any time.

Busting the Life Insurance Lies

Your term premiums are handled the same way. Your Paid-Up Addition contribution has a minimum and a maximum. I'll encourage you to make at least the minimum each month or each year, and while each insurance company has its own rules on PUA riders, with us you can essentially float between the minimum and maximum. Just don't go over the maximum, that will create a Modified Endowment Contract and reduce some of your tax benefits and flexibility. If you get to a place where you want to save more, we can always start an additional policy; lots of people do that as their earning power increases and they gain confidence watching their cash value grow.

"If you run into a period of slow cash flow, you can start by reducing the PUA contribution you're making, so you'll pay less without risking a premium payment. You can also borrow against your cash value to make the whole life premium payment. That's called an Automatic Premium Loan and can be done internally. It's just for the whole life, though, not for the term insurance or the PUA contributions. That same strategy can be used to access the cash value: you borrow against the cash value and pay the insurance company an interest rate to do so. We'll send you a check, and you can pay it back on your own schedule, though you want to stay on top of this, as you'll keep paying interest until the loan is paid back. Meanwhile, your own cash value, which you borrowed against, essentially using it for collateral for your policy loan, stays inside the policy and continues to grow and earn dividends.

"Alternatively, you can withdraw from your cash value and owe no interest, but then you can't put that money back in, and any withdrawals above what you've already put in will be subject to income tax."

Kara was furiously scribbling notes. "Okay, I think I get all that... basically we've got a lot of built-in flexibility. It sounds like these policies are designed to help us be able to pay for them!"

Evan grinned. "You're not far wrong there. We really want our clients to get the most out of their policies, and being confident they can make payments is important for that."

A few minutes and a couple more questions later, the papers were signed and Evan was walking the relieved couple back out to the lobby. "I want to tell you I'm pretty impressed, by the way," he said. "You've asked great questions and I can see you have done your homework. I wish half the people who come to talk to me knew half as much as you two about what they're looking for. Please know I'm available when you think of any more questions. You can email me or call and schedule another appointment anytime. I find people learn as they go with these policies, so we'll review them as your situation changes and grows and you learn more about how to actually use them."

***

Stephen and Kara are almost through. Let's take a look through some of the last few lies they're learning to bust.

Busting the Life Insurance Lies

Lie #18:
"PREMIUM" MEANS COST: YOU MAKE PAYMENTS AND NEVER SEE YOUR MONEY AGAIN!

The truth is that, in time, you will get back every penny and more that you put into a whole life insurance policy. That's because your premiums build an asset (your cash value) at a very competitive savings rate, while also creating an additional benefit to your heir(s) when you die. And that's if you make your premium payments and do nothing else. However, you can use your policy to gain back many multiples of your premiums sooner rather than later--while you're still alive to enjoy it.

Paying premiums (and Paid-Up Additions) to build that cash value is similar to paying money into a savings account. Most people assume that a dollar can only do one job at a time, or maybe two if you're lucky or a savvy investor. In everyday use, there's some truth in this: a dollar you use to buy a Double-Double at In'N'Out Burger is not a dollar you can save for college, or put toward a car payment, or donate to charity. A dollar in your bank account can be a savings fund and provide interest, so that's two jobs. But that's as many uses as most people think one dollar (or even a sum of many dollars) can have. And it's no wonder we think this way, as many financial products are set up to restrict the jobs a dollar can do! A 401(k) is for retirement dollars, a 529 is for college dollars, you may have a savings account for your emergency fund, a health savings account is for healthcare dollars, and so on.

The beauty of whole life insurance is that it allows the same dollar or dollars to do multiple jobs. One dollar paid into your whole life policy can actually perform seven jobs at once: pay the premium, build up cash value, create a waiver of premium rider, install the initial death benefit, provide the ability to leverage cash value through loans, increase the death benefit, and enable Paid-Up Additions. (Many of these we've already seen in this book; a few are still coming up!)

Those are all jobs your dollars can do inside of the policy, which might not get you too excited yet. What really makes a difference for your personal finances is how you can use your cash value dollars now to do multiple jobs inside of your personal economy as well! You no longer need to save in 10 different places for 10 reasons. Doing that is incredibly inefficient, because you can end up with dollars trapped in a 401(k) when you need a new roof, or money in a college savings account when your child announces they're leaving college to start a business.

But when you put dollars in a whole life policy, you have access to money you can use any time for any reason, because you can always leverage your cash value when emergencies OR opportunities arise.

Here's an example of what using your whole life policy to make dollars do multiple jobs can look like. Let's say a person wants to do an investment in a bridge loan (a highly secured type of loan) where he'll lend a colleague $250,000 at 12% interest. But he doesn't have a quarter of a million just lying around, so to fund this venture he takes out a bank loan at 4% interest, using the cash value of his life insurance policy as collateral. (Note: he could also have borrowed against his cash value at the insurance company instead.) His poli-

Busting the Life Insurance Lies

cy also provides 4% growth between cash value and dividends, so what he loses in loan interest he makes up through policy growth. So that's two uses of his life insurance dollars right there--loan collateral and growing cash value.

Plus, now that he has the bridge loan investment set up, his colleague will be paying him 12% interest back annually. 12% of $250,000 is $30,000. So not only are this man's life insurance dollars providing collateral and liquidity for him, they're also enabling him to make more money (a third use), which he can invest in a whole new income stream like a rental property, or use to increase the cash value of the policy (by adding to Paid-Up Additions) that let him do all of this in the first place.

And what happens when the bridge loan funds are repaid? Now those cash value dollars can be used as collateral for something else! Perhaps it's time to purchase a new car, remodel the kitchen, seek out a new investment, help a child with college tuition, or make a different business investment.

You can see now how paying a premium isn't just covering the cost of having a life insurance policy. It's the capital contribution to build a valuable, renewable, multi-use asset over time. And as that asset builds, there are a number of ways that you do in fact see your money again (and again), many of which we've touched on throughout this book so far:

- A significant amount of your premium payment goes directly to building your cash value.

- If you have a Paid-Up Additions (PUA) rider on your policy (as Evan explained in our story, this is a rider that allows you to make extra payments to grow your cash value faster), any additional payments you make go directly to your cash value as well.

- You can leverage your cash value for investments.

- The dollars in your cash value make the rest of your personal economy more efficient.

- The dividends your policy pays can come back to you as cash if you'd prefer not to put them back into the policy.

- Premiums also increase your death benefit dollars, raising the value of your estate.

- The death benefit doesn't give money to you, but it does give it to your beneficiary, which can enable you to use and spend other assets more productively. (See ProsperityPeaks.com/Permission for a special report about this.)

By allowing for all of these things, a whole life policy *optimizes* your dollars by letting them do multiple jobs at once. Plus, because whole life policies have a guaranteed cash value and a guaranteed increase, your cash value will always grow, and will eventually compound to be much higher than the sum of the premiums you put into the policy. In time, you will always get more out of a policy than you put into it.

(For illustrations of how premiums grow both the cash value and death benefit in whole life policies, see Appendices B and C of this book. Notice some illustrations have PUA's while some don't so that you can compare.)

Lie #19:
IF YOU CAN'T PAY YOUR PREMIUMS, YOU'RE IN SERIOUS TROUBLE

This is a legitimate fear for a lot of people. In most contexts, missing a payment (let alone several payments) on anything is very scary. Missed payments in other areas of life can mean hefty fines, interest rate hikes, ruined credit, turned-off utility services, repossessed cars, eviction notices, and the like. These are scary things that no one ever wants to have to deal with! So it's natural for people to fear that if they can't pay their insurance premiums for a little while, they'll lose all their money *and* their insurance policy.

Fortunately, whole life insurance premiums aren't nearly as strict as some people make them out to be. While a policy could be canceled in a worst-case scenario, there are plenty of options to keep it going and in force if you're struggling to pay your premium or have to miss a couple payments.

If your policy is already quite mature, say over 15 years old, you could consider what's called a natural vanish. A natural vanish allows you to stop paying premiums entirely once your policy reaches a certain level of maturity. If you've been utilizing your maximum Paid-Up Additions, this option may be available to you around 7-10 years on your policy. If you don't have any Paid-Up Additions, natural vanish will be an option around 17-20 years. Either way, your dividends (if you have a participating policy), your cash value, and your death benefit all remain intact.

If your policy is eligible to receive dividends, you can put your dividend toward paying the premium. This is another great option for more mature policies since the dividend is typically more substantial by then.

If you started your policy with an annual payment, but that lump sum isn't workable for you now, you can switch to a monthly payment. This allows you to spread the payments out and chip away at it a little at a time. You can actually change your payment schedule between annual and monthly as needed throughout the entire duration of your policy. (Note: all insurance companies charge a small amount to pay monthly because your cash value is the same whether you pay annually or monthly. The insurance company is essentially lending you the annual premium while you pay them back monthly, so there will be a small fee to pay monthly.)

You can borrow against your cash value to pay your policy premiums. This is called an automatic premium loan, and while you'll be trading premium payments for interest-bearing loan payments, it may be a good tradeoff for you because the timing of the loan payments is up to you.

If you don't believe you could pay back a policy loan within a few years, or you don't want to incur interest, you can simply withdraw the necessary amount from your cash value. This option, however, should only be taken as a last resort. Once you actually withdraw cash value, that cash value can't be put back, whereas with a loan, you can "put the money back" by paying the loan back.

If cash flow problems won't go away, you can *partially* reduce your policy's death benefit, thereby reducing the premiums (and the Paid-Up Addition capability). This is a good solution if you just don't see cash flow rising ever again. Once you reduce the policy, you can't bring it back up again, but you can keep contributing by paying the premium at its new lower amount.

Another possibility is to choose a *"reduced paid-up"* option. This means that your death benefit (not your cash value) will be reduced to permanently pay off your policy. Your premium payments will be gone for good in exchange for a lowered death benefit. This is a good option if you want to get rid of your payments entirely in one fell swoop but still want to keep your cash value. But it is a permanent change that can't be undone, so give it some thought before choosing this route.

Then there's one thing you can do that doesn't actually involve making any alterations to the policy itself: try rearranging your cash flow. For example, if there's a way to reduce your debt, perhaps even by leveraging your cash value to pay off high-interest debt, or by lowering your retirement contributions to your 401(k), you may be able to find some extra wiggle room in your budget for your policy premium. You can also look at your budget and find ways to reduce your spending.

So really, there are many ways to tailor your policy to your situation in any given moment. As long as you keep the insurance company and/or the advisor apprised of your situation and enlist their help in making whatever policy changes you need, you should be just fine-- even if you need to miss a payment or two.

(See Appendix E for partially reduced and reduced paid up illustrations.)

Lie #20:

IF YOU BORROW AGAINST YOUR POLICY, YOU'RE PAYING TO BORROW YOUR OWN MONEY

Well that doesn't sound fair! No one wants to borrow their own money, let alone pay someone else to do it. Fortunately, that's not actually how life insurance loans work.

If you take out a life insurance loan, you're *not* borrowing your own money. You're borrowing against your cash value, from the insurance company's pool of capital. The company uses your money as collateral on the loan, so your money doesn't actually go anywhere. This pool of capital (made up of all premiums paid into the company, less operating costs and dividends) is what the insurance company uses to invest and make money for itself. It also provides a tremendous benefit for policyholders by giving them access to capital.

Now, you might think that borrowing money from *anywhere* sounds like a bad idea…but there are some great reasons to borrow from a life insurance company when you need money. You can avoid the stress of trying to qualify to borrow money in between jobs, if the economy is down, or when lender standards have suddenly tightened. You don't have to borrow for an "acceptable" or approved reason. You won't have your credit history examined, nor will there be inquiries or a loan reported on your credit. You can design a flexible repayment schedule, and of course, there are never any prepayment penalties. And you won't get charged with late payment penalties, double digit interest rates, or annual fees.

Another advantage is often overlooked, but it's an important consideration. When you know you can borrow against your savings, doesn't that to make it easier to save? There's nothing more important to building financial security than saving money, but when we're not sure we can use our savings if an emergency (or an opportunity) arises, we tend to scrimp on saving money. Whole life helps us save by helping us increase our liquidity, and being able to borrow against our savings is key.

When you exercise this benefit and borrow, the company charges interest because they no longer have as much in their investing pool. If you have a participating policy, some of that interest will find its way back to you in the form of dividends. Remember that as a policy owner, you have an ownership interest in the company. You want them to be profitable because with a mutual (think of it as "mutually owned") company, the profits are distributed to the policyowners (you!) as dividends. The dividends are not guaranteed, but many mutual companies have paid them every single year for over 150 years--even through the Great Depression--so they are extremely reliable! Whether you take advantage of loans yourself or not, you are participating in a very sound and proven business model that pays consistent dividends.

This strategy works out for everyone. The life insurance company still earns money, you use their money to keep yours growing in your account, and the other policyholders trust that the company is investing their money wisely. It's a win-win-win situation. And it's interesting to note here that insurance companies get much of their highly reliable dividend-paying ability from their business model of providing products that require steady inflow (premiums), rather than from great investment skills.

Lie #21:
YOU HAVE TO BORROW TO ACCESS THE MONEY, WHICH CUTS CASH VALUE GROWTH

This isn't so much a lie as it is just confusion about the different ways you can access your money in a whole life policy. In many situations, borrowing against your cash value is the best option, but it's by no means the only option. If you want to access your cash value without borrowing, you can simply withdraw it. These withdrawals are tax-free until you reach the basis of the policy, the total amount you've put in yourself. You *can* withdraw more than that--you can even withdraw almost your entire cash value if you want--but you'll have to pay income tax on those further withdrawals. This is one reason people use policy loans instead of withdrawals, assuming they can pay the loans back to begin with.

This is also a lie because it says borrowing reduces your cash value growth. Not true. Borrowing is so highly recommended because it allows your cash value to actually stay in your policy where it keeps growing, guaranteed, every year (even if no dividends are paid). Remember, the money you get in your loan actually belongs to the insurance company, and your cash value acts as collateral for that loan. That means your money grows at the same rate (or a very close rate if you have a direct recognition policy, which we'll talk about in a later lie) because the full amount of cash value is still there. The

Busting the Life Insurance Lies

growth on your cash value continues uninterrupted, even when you have accessed that value through a policy loan.

Also, remember that mutual whole life policies almost always yield dividends--the insurance company's profits that come back to you as a policyholder. As noted above, dividends aren't guaranteed to be paid, but historically they are highly reliable. Most major mutual companies have paid dividends consistently for over 100 plus years. Dividends may not yield as large lump sum amounts as either borrowing or withdrawing can get you, but they are highly flexible. You can choose to put the received money called dividends toward your premiums, toward your cash value (via an automatic PUA rider), or directly into your pocket. Depending on how much money you need, these options for your dividends may offset the need for either policy loans or withdrawals.

And these are only a few of the options you have for getting cash from your whole life policy. Others include:

- Receiving an accelerated death benefit (part of your DB, awarded to you while you're still alive)

- Selling your policy outright

- Borrowing against your death benefit (available only for elderly people)

- Annuitizing your policy (turning it into a cash-generating vehicle that pays you directly)

- Turning your policy into a charitable remainder trust (where a charity receives your death benefit and pays you a regular income until you die)

These are less common, more complex, and often last resort or end-of-life options for obtaining cash from your whole life policy. Between borrowing, withdrawing, and cash dividends, you may never need any of them. But they are viable paths, and a qualified insurance advisor can help you set up any of them if they appeal to you or become necessary.

All in all, borrowing against cash value isn't the only way to get money from your policy. But oftentimes it is the best way. You get money in your pocket while your cash value keeps growing for you to use in the future. That's a pretty big benefit that won't happen if you just withdraw the money.

Lie #22:

I CAN ONLY COUNT ON THE GUARANTEED COLUMN (NOT DIVIDENDS)

Raise your hand if the name George Zimmer rings a bell.

No? Never heard of him? Ah, but you've probably *heard* him, even if you didn't know it at the time. Zimmer is the former president and CEO of The Men's Wearhouse, and became widely known for ending that company's commercials by saying "I guarantee it." (You can hear him saying it in your mind now, can't you?)

Guarantees are to the professional world what pinky-promises were in kindergarten: ironclad vows you know you can count on. So it's understandable that with an insurance policy, when you see something that looks like this, you might get a little confused (see Appendices A, B, C, and D).

Why do whole life policies have two columns that aren't guaranteed? And more importantly, why would you, the policy owner, even look at those other two columns? Why wouldn't you focus only on what's guaranteed? That's all you can really count on, right?

Well, not quite.

The difference between the guaranteed and non-guaranteed columns in a whole life policy are determined by dividends. One non-guaranteed column shows what will happen if maximum dividends (according to current rates) are produced by a participating policy and then paid into the policy to further grow its cash value; the second column shows what would happen if the dividends produce at 50% of that maximum.

Clearly if you have a non-participating policy (one that doesn't produce dividends), this is a non-issue. But in a participating policy, it brings up the question behind this lie: how can you count on dividends enough to assume that a policy will actually deliver returns like the ones in its non-guaranteed columns?

Here's the thing. Mutual insurance companies have been paying dividends consistently, without fail, for over 150 years. During the Great Depression, they paid dividends. During the economic issues of the late 1970s, they paid dividends. During the Great Recession of 2008 and 2009, when the rest of the country was losing its collective shirt in the stock market, mutual insurance companies paid record amounts of dividends to their policy owners. So while technically it is *possible* to have a participating whole life policy that fails to pay you dividends, it's pretty much never happened. Could yours be the first? Sure, possibly...but we doubt it will be.

If you're still skeptical, here's something you can absolutely count on: any dividends paid to your policy become a part of its guaranteed cash value. This creates a new floor of cash value in your policy which will never go back down (unless you withdraw it, or borrow against it and don't repay). And by raising the cash value, these dividends cause the death benefit to increase as well. It's the opposite of a vicious circle. And it's guaranteed.

Speaking of guarantees, competitors to whole life advisors (usually financial planners and stockbrokers) love to try comparing their accounts with the guarantees of whole life. They point to their interest rates, their historical growth, their projections, etc., and compare those things to whole life's guaranteed column, saying that there's no way a whole life policy can keep pace with their investment assets. And they're good at saying it. It's one of the main reasons so many people ran from whole life to mutual funds in the 1980s and 1990s.

But here's what they don't tell you. In reality, there's only one "guarantee" the stock market can give you: -100% return. That's *negative one hundred percent*. In other words, unless you're using leverage (in which case you can lose more), the most you can lose is everything you've invested. Not much of a guarantee, is it? Stockbrokers and financial planners often like to say they can guarantee 0% return, meaning you'll keep your original stake no matter what, but really, they can't guarantee that high. If you invest $100,000 in an investment tied to the stock market, the only guarantee around that money is that you could lose all of it. And if you add in more money or grow it over time until you have $150,000 or more, you could still lose it all.

Will that actually happen to you? Maybe, maybe not. It happened to a lot of people in 2008, especially investors--and banks--who leveraged their investments. Yes, a lot of people have lost less than their stake in the stock market, and many have made money as well. The point here isn't that you'll *automatically* lose money in the stock market. The point is that no matter what a stockbroker or financial planner selling mutual funds tells you, their industry has *no other guarantees*. Everything else is speculation.

A whole life policy guarantees a death benefit. It guarantees premiums that will never rise. It guarantees a cash value that will only ever go up until and unless you withdraw from it. It guarantees that the profits of the mutual company (over and above costs and required reserves) will be distributed to the policyholders in the form of dividends. It guarantees any dividends that are paid and reinvested in the policy will grow that cash value. It guarantees cash value that you can borrow against. And it guarantees your savings won't be lost in a market crash, and that your gains are locked in, forever. For our money, that's a much better choice.

Lie #23:
SHORT PAY POLICIES ARE PREFERABLE TO LONGER-PAY OPTIONS

Short pay policies are policies that contain your premiums within a shorter timeframe than regular full-pay whole life. Various short pay policies have payments over only 10 or 20 years, for example. These policies can have a certain appeal, since knowing that your premiums will disappear after a certain point can bring peace of mind.

But here's our question: if a product is good, why limit your ability to contribute to it? If you're going to get a policy, why not get one that focuses on building a lifelong emergency/opportunity fund for you--and that allows you to pay into that fund for the rest of your life? We recommend you keep paying premiums and contributing to your PUAs as long as you are earning work-related income, because as long as you are earning cash - or your investments are earning cash - you've got to have a place to safely store and grow that cash. And as too many people learned in the last stock market downturn, the market is a terrible place to "save" (ahem, gamble) money in your later years. So don't limit the "bucket" that holds your cash!

Plus, you don't have to get a short pay policy to stop paying your premium after a certain time. Recall again the natural vanish option we talked about in Lie #19. This option makes your premiums stop being required after 10 or 20 years as well, but it also allows you to keep paying premiums and PUAs if you desire.

Remember, most of your payments fund your cash value, which grows your death benefit and serves as an asset you can leverage. And once you get past the third year or so of paying premiums and maximum PUAs (or the seventh year without maximum PUAs), you'll see that every premium paid generates an equal increase in cash value. Most of your PUA dollars have the same effect.

So if you limit your payment ability to just a few years, you limit your own ability to build cash value and maximize your death benefit over the rest of your life. We don't recommend it.

Lie #24:
YOU DON'T BREAK EVEN UNTIL THE 20TH YEAR OF PAYING FOR YOUR POLICY

This is one of the biggest payment questions we get. Because paying whole life premiums can represent a significant amount of money, many people want to know how soon that premium stream is going to break even. And it's a common misconception that for a whole life insurance policy, it takes at least 20 years.

Part of the confusion in this lie comes from the fact that there are actually two different ways to break even:

- *Cumulative* break even, which means that your total cash value equals your total contributions to date (year 1 plus year 2 plus year 3, etc.). This typically happens around year 7 with maximum PUAs, and in year 14-19 without.

- *Annual* break even, which means that in any given year, your cash value increases by the amount you paid in that year (or more). If maximum PUAs have been applied, this can happen as early as year 3 or 4; if not, it usually happens by year 10 or 11.

(For an illustration of these two ways to break even, see Appendix B1.)

Depending on how much you've been able to contribute in Paid-Up Additions, between year 3 and year 7 of policy ownership (give or take) you will start to see all of your premiums and most of your PUAs go directly to cash value. This allows the policy to start ap-

Kim D. H. Butler and Jack Burns

proaching both cumulative and annual break even as early as immediately, but rarely later than 6 or 7 years out.

Put another way, it only takes a few years until you "get back every dollar" that you put into the policy each year, especially if you maximize your Paid-Up Additions. In the meantime, you've also secured a permanent death benefit and you are building an asset you can leverage if needed or wanted, and it's hard to calculate the value of that. And while getting to cumulative break even does take some time, and depends somewhat on how much you're able to pay in PUAs, it won't take you 20 years. It may even take less than 5 years.

Lie #25:
A WHOLE LIFE POLICY WITHOUT PAID-UP ADDITIONS IS WORTHLESS

We brought up Paid-Up Additions (PUAs) in this section's narrative, when Evan explained their use to Stephen and Kara. PUAs are a great way to grow your cash value higher and faster if you're able to make them--not unlike paying your surplus income into a savings account at the end of every month or year. Like Evan did, we'd recommend maximizing your PUAs every year that you can, so that you have more cash value to borrow against and you have it sooner. This can be especially helpful in the first few years of the policy, when cash value hasn't had a chance to grow much yet just from premium payments. PUAs can give it some extra juice while the premiums get up to speed.

That being said, a whole life policy doesn't *have* to have a PUA rider to be a good policy. We've actually seen a few insurance advisors cancel perfectly good policies just because they didn't have PUAs set up. This was totally unnecessary--not only were the policies fine to begin with, the policy owners now had to deal with the inefficient first few years of slowly building cash value again. Not a good strategy.

The disadvantage of a non-PUA policy is simply that it takes a little longer to build up cash value, since as we've seen, the first few years of premiums pay more to commissions and up-front costs than to cash value. For this reason, in the short term this kind of policy is not a great place to store cash the way most whole life policies are. But once you get past the short term, a whole life policy will build cash value steadily and deliver competitive returns whether it has PUA contributions or not. It's not a bad policy at all. In fact, if you're starting a policy very young (or for someone very young), skipping the PUAs won't make much difference--and may even ease the initial financial burden of starting the policy.

So while PUAs can be important and very helpful, and we generally recommend them, you wouldn't want to get rid of a whole life policy just because it didn't have them.

***

A much relieved and reassured Kara shook Evan's hand once more and walked to the elevator beside her husband.

Stephen laced his fingers with hers. "Hey there, love. Feeling okay? I think this was a good decision, don't you?"

She smiled, pressing one hand to her still-flat stomach. "Definitely. Little one here is going to be really taken care of now. And so are we."

"Absolutely," he agreed. "Now let me take you to lunch before we both need to get back to work."

Kara grinned up at him. "It's a date."

The couple walked out into the late morning sunlight, holding hands.

Busting the Life Insurance Lies

Kim D. H. Butler and Jack Burns

Part 5:

"PRO-WHOLE-LIFE" LIES, THE ADVISOR'S PERSPECTIVE, AND THE REST OF THE STORY

As we were writing this book, it became clear to us that in a certain light, it could read like a giant sales letter for whole life insurance, painting a glorious picture of a product that might just be too good to be true. And while we do believe whole life is a fantastic option for many people (and a better option than many of its alternatives and competitors), we don't want to mislead anyone by offering only one side of the story. So we've endeavored thus far to be as evenhanded as possible, to point out where other forms of insurance can be valuable (starting a term policy for immediate coverage, for instance), and to show how a whole life policy is not some kind of infinite free money generator (yes, you have to pay premiums and keep up with loan payments when you use whole life). In this section, we're going to go a couple steps further.

We'll start by making what may be a surprising admission: *not all lies in the insurance industry are anti-whole-life*. There are a number of lies out there that actually make whole life seem better than it is. These pro-whole-life lies have no more place in the insurance indus-

Busting the Life Insurance Lies

try than any of the others we've discussed so far. By busting these lies, we not only present the most realistic view of whole life, we also allow you, the reader, to make the most informed decision possible.

We also want to take a few minutes to share why we love the life insurance industry so much. So we've created one more character for Kara and Stephen to meet; he's not exactly either of us, but he's loosely based on elements of our experiences. We hope you enjoy meeting him as well!

***

THREE MONTHS LATER...

Stephen saved the spreadsheet he was working on, stretched, and then reached under his desk for his lunch. After a week of rain, it was finally warm and bright enough to eat lunch outside again, and he'd been itching to get out in the sun since he drove in that morning.

He'd just settled himself on a bench at the park across the street when his cell phone started playing Queen's "Crazy Little Thing Called Love," the ringtone he'd given Kara's number when they became a couple back in college.

"Hi, love," he said, unwrapping a roast beef sandwich. "I just got out to the park for lunch, want to come meet me?"

"Love to, but I'm on my way to see Dr. Harper. Checkup today, remember?" Kara sounded tired but pleased.

"Oh yeah, you did tell me that this morning. The last few have gone well, so this one should too, right?"

"Yep, that's the plan," Kara said. "But that's not what I wanted to tell you."

"Oh?" Stephen asked, swallowing a bite of dill pickle. "What's up then?"

"Do you remember my Uncle Carl? My mom's oldest brother? He wasn't at Thanksgiving last year, but I'm pretty sure you've met him...maybe the year before, or something like that."

"I think so," Stephen said, popping open his can of root beer. "Big guy, used to be in the Navy, played cribbage with your brother David, liked to tease your mom about how she and Grandpa Bill got together?"

"I...how do you do that? I swear, you remember him better than I do!" Even after almost eight years together, Kara occasionally forgot about her husband's uncanny memory for people.

Stephen laughed. "Everyone's got one useless talent, hon. What about Uncle Carl?"

"Well, he just called me out of the blue. He's in town and he wants to take us to dinner tonight. And he was kinda mysterious about it, too. He said he'd talked to Mom and Dad, and wanted to tell us something that's still kind of a secret."

"Huh." Stephen munched his sandwich thoughtfully. "I didn't know he was in this area...isn't he running your granddad's construction company with his other brother a couple states over?"

"That's what I thought, too. But when I asked him, he said he'd tell us the whole story tonight. That's all I could get out of him, except to meet him at Bertucci's at seven."

"Well that's good enough for me!" Stephen cracked. "If you think I'm going to turn down Bertucci's osso buco and a mysterious story, you can think again."

Busting the Life Insurance Lies

Kara laughed. "I thought you might say that. See you at home, then. Love you."

"Love you back."

Carl Parsons was waiting for them at a quiet table near the back of the restaurant. As Stephen had remembered, Carl was tall and powerfully built, but his embrace for Kara was gentle. Once they had ordered, he turned to the young couple and smiled.

"I guess you're wondering what the big secret is that I wouldn't tell you on the phone," he said. Kara and Stephen nodded. "Well, you may remember that I stepped in to help my brother Jim run Parsons Construction when Dad--my dad, Kara's granddad, that is--passed about ten years ago." More nods. "Did you know what I did before that?"

Kara traded glances with her husband. "Actually, no. I know you were in the Navy, and in sales for a while, but I don't know much more than that. I guess I never asked."

Carl waved away her guilty look. "That's alright. No reason you should have. What I did was sell life insurance. And the big secret is that I'm about to start doing it again."

"What about the construction company?" asked Stephen.

"Sold it just a few weeks ago," said Carl with satisfaction. "You may as well know that wasn't my first interest. I stepped in when Dad died because Jim and Mom asked me to, and it was a family business, and I was the best choice at the time. And it wasn't a bad job at all. We did some great work there, built up a reputation anyone would be proud of. But it was never what I really loved."

"And you loved selling insurance?" Kara wondered aloud.

"The short answer to that is yes, I did. Still do. But more than that, I love what insurance allows people to do. You know, our family got really lucky that Dad didn't die ten or twelve years earlier. He'd have given his right arm for insurance, but he was uninsurable by the time he started getting sick. If he hadn't been able to build up the business to where it was when he passed, there would have been nothing left. We'd have had to sell the business for pennies on the dollar. We'd probably have gone bankrupt. And I know those first few years, especially when he had his first bypass surgery, Dad was really afraid he'd die before he'd created security for all of us. When I came in to fill in for him, I remember Mom telling me how relieved she was that he lived to see as much success as he did."

Kara shook her head slowly. "I didn't know any of this."

"No reason for you to. During the difficult times, you were still pretty young, and your parents had their own jobs. Once I came on board and things started turning around, there wasn't a need to tell everyone we'd gone through the rough patch. Plus, you kids already missed your granddad enough. We didn't want you worrying about money as well."

Stephen took a sip of wine. "That makes sense. I'm curious though, how did you go from selling insurance to running a big construction company and do so well? There can't be that much overlap between those two jobs."

"Well, there was and there wasn't," Carl continued. "You're right that I didn't know construction well. That was Jim's background, not mine. We were fortunate to have some great managers and foremen to help me get up to speed, plus some of the best sales associates in the business. But what helped me the most was that selling insurance had taught me how to work with people. And that was my biggest strength."

Busting the Life Insurance Lies

"What do you mean?" asked Kara. "Working with people how?"

"The most important thing I learned selling insurance is that people respond incredibly well when you do what you say you're going to do. That's why most life insurance companies got through the economic downturn so well, actually--the majority of them always do exactly what they say they will do. And that was something Jim and I had both learned from our dad--he never let us forget that one, let me tell you." Carl grinned, remembering, as their food arrived.

"I smell a story behind that last statement of yours, Carl," said Stephen, cutting into his osso buco.

"Oh, there are quite a few," Carl said. "Kara, did your mom ever tell you about the time he made me mow the lawn after midnight one Saturday?"

Kara looked up from her fettuccine. "No! What happened? Why did he do that?"

"I was supposed to have mowed it late that afternoon, but I sneaked off to meet my girlfriend instead. When I got back that night, Dad met me at the door and said I had to do it right then and there. He stood on the porch steps with a flashlight until I was done. Jim, the little rat, had already done his chores, and he about fell off the porch laughing at me."

"I bet you never made that mistake again!" said Stephen, who had almost choked on his wine laughing.

"No sir!" said Carl. "I think I mowed the lawn first thing in the morning every Saturday after that! And Jim had his share of times to learn that lesson from our dad, too. So when I stepped in at Parsons Construction, Jim and I made sure that stayed the #1 goal: we as a company would always do what we said we'd do. That helped make up for a lot of my own knowledge gap at first, since it let me

133   Kim D. H. Butler and Jack Burns

learn what we could do and how to make sure it got done well. After a couple years it made our reputation rock-solid. By seven years in, we barely needed to sign contracts anymore. Clients trusted us so much they'd just send us the money and say okay, let's get started.

"The second thing I learned is that if you want to be successful, you have to care about people. For the most part, life insurance advisors care deeply about their clients--they have to these days, after how much the industry gets trashed in the media for a few loudmouths selling gimmicky products and taking huge commissions. Every advisor I'm still in touch with from my insurance days doesn't give a damn about the size of their commission as long as their client gets exactly what is best for that client. They care more about the clients than the clients care about themselves, most of the time. Believe it or not, it can be hard to get some people to consider their own best interests, or even what's best for the people they love the most.

"Incidentally, the advisor you're working with, Evan Holmes? One of the advisors I'm still in touch with is his dad, Ethan. We worked at the same company for several years, and he was one of the ones who truly cared. When he retired, something like five hundred people came to his farewell dinner. I remember one time he got a call for advice from a family friend who had a term policy that was about to expire. Ethan knew that there was another term policy he could sell this friend that would net him a commission. But what the guy really needed was to convert the term to a whole life policy, so that's what Ethan told him to do. He didn't make a cent on that deal. But he did it because it was the right thing for that person."

Stephen and Kara were rapt, their food forgotten as they listened.

"So I took that care with me to Parsons, and not just for our clients, for our employees. There's a lot of turnover in construction, but Parsons had about half the usual rate. We invested so much care in our

Busting the Life Insurance Lies

people that they didn't want to leave. We always erred on the side of giving them too much rather than too little, and they wanted to give their best work in return."

Carl stopped to take a drink of water, then smiled at his captive audience.

"The last big thing I learned," said Carl, "is that there's something about life insurance that makes me feel good on a personal level. I loved what we were able to accomplish at Parsons, but I felt like I was doing more good for more people out on the street selling life insurance than I ever was building buildings. That I can bring a different perspective to it now from ten years building a construction company is just icing on the cake, so to speak."

There was a short silence as the couple took everything in. Then Stephen leaned forward.

"That's all really inspiring, Carl. I'm speechless, and that's saying something." Kara giggled in spite of herself, and Stephen grinned at her. "But here's where I'm a little lost: why did you invite us out to dinner to tell us about it? You're not from here, and you haven't seen Kara or me in a couple years. You could have emailed, or called, or put the news in one of those fancy holiday update letters like my mom sends out every year. Why tell us, and why do it this way?"

Carl gave him a knowing smile. "I wondered if you'd catch on to that. I did this the way I did it because I'm not going to sell life insurance in the town where Parsons Construction was. I'm going to sell it here. I moved here last week. Ethan is helping me get situated--he still lives here and does a little selling part-time."

"That's great!" said Kara. "It'll be good to have you closer. You can meet your grandniece or grandnephew soon."

"Right," agreed Carl. "Definitely looking forward to that!"

"So now that you're here...should we start getting our insurance policies from you?" Stephen asked. "We got started with Evan, as you know, but I'm sure we could switch over somehow."

"No, no," Carl said. "Evan is perfect for who you are and where you are--plus you've already started with him and I know you're in good hands, so I wouldn't feel right poaching you from him. Evan's your man. Don't worry about me, I'll make out just fine."

Kara nodded. "That makes sense. I'm still glad you'll be in town, though. We've got a lot of years to catch up on."

"We sure do," said Carl. "Now let's order dessert and you can tell me how things with the baby are going..."

***

Everything Carl Parsons said about life insurance is exactly how we feel about it. Working in this industry has been an honor and a pleasure for us both, and we believe it's the best and most helpful industry out there. We hope you enjoyed hearing a dramatized version of our story as much as we enjoyed telling it.

Now let's look at some of these pro-whole-life lies, so you can get a balanced picture of whole life going forward.

Busting the Life Insurance Lies

Lie #26:
YOU SHOULD PUT ALL YOUR MONEY INTO A WHOLE LIFE POLICY

We've talked a lot about how a whole life policy can be a good alternative to things like bank savings accounts, CDs, money market accounts, etc. We've also talked about how whole life is a lot steadier and more reliable than anything backed by the stock market. So by now you might be thinking "wow, what I really need to do is close out my investments and other accounts, get a whole life policy, and move all my money there right now!"

That's actually not a good move. Remember, a whole life policy is not an investment, it's a place to store cash over time, as well as a way to put permanent protection in place for your Human Life Value. It's a fantastic diversification tool as well, and it's an asset you can borrow against to meet emergencies or opportunities you wouldn't be able to fund otherwise. But while it does those specific things very well, a whole life policy won't necessarily be the best tool to meet every financial goal you may have.

The cash value of your policy does grow significantly over time, but the goal of its growth is to increase your emergency/opportunity fund. So if you have other investments, draining all of them to put massive amounts of money into a whole life policy won't improve your financial situation. In fact, it will probably make it worse--especially since many investments get hit with a hefty tax and/or penalty when you withdraw their cash early. Plus, some kinds of investments don't transfer to insurance at all. IRA money and qualified retirement plan money are both unacceptable for insurance policy premiums. So while you could theoretically liquidate your 401(k) or 403(b) to put the cash in a life insurance policy, it would be an inefficient use of your dollars and poor financial advice.

Also, remember that insurance is built up and paid into over time. Most whole life policies have limits on how much can be paid in annually, and tax penalties for paying in too much at once. (Lie #33 talks more about one of these limits, called a MEC.) So whole life isn't a great solution for a large, sudden windfall or an IRA rollover where you're trying to invest--or reinvest--a large chunk of money at once.

So instead of taking all your money out of wherever it is and putting it toward a whole life policy, we strongly encourage you to play the long game and build up your policy over time. You will want to pay your annual or monthly premiums, and you should pay your maximum Paid-Up Additions annually if you can, but that's all you need to do, and it's also the best way for your policy to be funded. (And your policy can keep growing without paying either of those after a certain amount of time--remember the "natural vanish" option from lie #19.)

One time this lie is close to a truth is when you are just getting started with investing, or when you haven't even yet begun. You see, it's critical to save and establish your financial foundation first, before you begin investing. Many people start putting money into their 401(k)s as soon as possible, but they have no emergency fund, and no savings! Then when the roof needs to be fixed or some other major expense comes along, they have to withdraw from their 401(k) or IRA, paying penalties and taxes, perhaps even liquidating when the market is low. And this is a significant trend today. In 2015, one in eight Americans withdrew money from a retirement fund to pay for unexpected expenses or emergencies, because they had only the retirement investment vehicle, not any other emergency fund saved up. Ouch!

We recommend saving first. And a whole life policy is the perfect place for that. It builds your foundation (cash value) as well as protection (death benefit, as well as riders like Long Term Care and Waiver of Premium). Then you can invest with security, knowing that your income is protected and you have an adequate emergency fund of six to twelve months of living expenses. This way you don't have to raid your investments or go into debt when emergencies come along.

And if you are just getting started, you also need to save for opportunities, too, so that you have money to invest with! Many clients will save, for instance, $50k or $100k in their policies, and then use that money to help them purchase a rental home or invest elsewhere (only in places where they are assured they can earn a higher rate of return than the cost of borrowing against their cash value.) Then they rinse and repeat, using their savings to build their investments.

Yes, some people do use their whole life policies as their main financial strategy, but as you probably realize by now, there are ways to use your policy to generate even better results. Once your policy's cash value is built up, borrow against it to cover emergencies or fund opportunities. That's its main function aside from the death benefit: being an asset that stores your cash until you need it or want it.

This leads us to the next two pro-whole-life lies, both of which are about what a whole life policy can and can't do for you. (See Appendix G).

Lie #27:

A WHOLE LIFE POLICY PROVIDES REGULAR INCOME TO FUND YOUR DAILY NEEDS

This is one of those lies that's true in very specific situations, but *only* in those situations, so if you assume it will automatically apply to you, you'll be in trouble.

If you are over 80 and started your policy when you were in your 20s or 30s, there are ways to convert it to an income stream that will likely fund the rest of your life's day-to-day needs. You could convert the policy to an immediate annuity (an investment that pays you a regular income stream), for instance, or change your dividends to come to you as cash payments. Either of those options could provide regular income for you at that point. But what enables either of those options is the fact that your cash value has been growing for over *fifty years*.

If you are younger than about 75, those options will typically not work well for you no matter when you started the policy--there's just not enough value in it yet for those tactics to provide a viable income stream for another 20 years of living (give or take). You might find that your policy dividends can provide some helpful supplementary income, but you're not likely to be living off of your policy.

If you're starting a whole life policy in your 50s or 60s, you won't have time to build up enough cash value to provide income options for yourself even by the time you're in your 80s and 90s, unless you

Busting the Life Insurance Lies

140

are able to fund it very aggressively. (This is an area that requires a competent life insurance advisor to navigate; they'll be able to tell you specifically where your cutoff for those options is and why it's there.)

Now you may be wondering, "But even if I can't annuitize my policy or convert my dividends to cash, I can still borrow against my policy for income, right?"

Technically, yes...but we wouldn't recommend that, if you're not planning on paying it back. In earlier years of life (before 75ish), if you try to borrow against your cash value for annual income, you'll simply create too large of a loan that you or your death benefit will need to pay back with interest. If you don't have reliable income to begin with, that's the *last* thing you want to do. We'd only recommend something like this if you're using the loan to provide support for an actual venture, like starting a business or a solid cash-flowing investment. If all you want or need is an income stream, taking after-tax withdrawals may be a better strategy than borrowing.

In later years (after 75ish), borrowing to create income has issues as well. As you continue to borrow, you create an interest expense on top of the need to pay the loan back, both of which grow every year. The task of paying those back will fall on your death benefit--if you're lucky. If you die "on time," the death benefit will cover any outstanding loans and interest before it gets awarded to your beneficiary. But if you don't die "on time," the policy could implode--fall apart from the inside due to high interest expense. In that event, you'd be taxed for all the policy growth above your own contributions in one year as if it were income--which, by that point in time, would be a *lot* of money. You don't want to gamble on that!

So we really recommend keeping your whole life policy in its role an emergency/opportunity fund. Not only is that what it's meant to do, it avoids a number of serious potential pitfalls. Whole life policies are extremely flexible financial tools, but if incoming cash flow is your main and only need, whole life might not necessarily be the best strategy. (However, in some situations, they might be used to *fund* the perfect strategy, so don't despair, just get some guidance to understand your options.)

Lie #28:

A WHOLE LIFE POLICY MEANS YOU DON'T NEED ANY OTHER INVESTMENTS

After everything we've said about other investments, especially ones that are tied to the stock market, it may come as a surprise to see this lie here--or even that it's a lie at all. Here's the thing: we don't have anything against these other investment vehicles *in and of themselves*. Our objections largely come from the ways that whole life insurance is held up to them as a bad alternative by people trying to sell mutual funds or stock and bond accounts. Remember, whole life is not an investment. It's an asset that stores and grows cash while protecting your Human Life Value. It doesn't grow money only for retirement, it builds an emergency/opportunity fund. It doesn't speculate, it guarantees. Comparing it to a stock market vehicle is literally like comparing apples and tennis balls--they're not even similar enough to be apples and oranges!

This issue here is not that investing is bad, but that investing for growth or even cash flow before (or instead of) establishing security through a whole life policy doesn't make sense. Remember the idea of self-insurance we talked about in Lie #7? If your investments do grow, you'll make some money, but if they don't, you could have nothing to fall back on. And even if your investments do well, chances are, they're not liquid, you can't use them as collateral, and they're not sufficient to self-insure your Human Life Value.

What we advise is to get your emergency/opportunity fund established *first*. For our money, whole life is the best way to do that. Especially in the early years of life (teens, 20s, and 30s), saving money is paramount--so if you can only afford one vehicle for saving or storing your cash during that time, we encourage you to make it a whole life policy. If you are well beyond your 30's, with or without investments, it's still never too late to build your financial foundation. Whether you are 25 or 65, you'll still encounter unexpected expenses that will set you back again and again if you don't have adequate savings.

But once you've built up the policy into a workable emergency/opportunity fund, or once you can make your premiums and PUAs with money left over, by all means invest! In fact, if your goal at that point is to invest for growth of capital, and you want to achieve double digit growth with no loss of principle (a good rule of thumb for investing), whole life actually *isn't* your best bet. There have been some years of double digit gross dividends in whole life's history, but it's not the norm. Similarly, if your investment goal is cash flow to live on, whole life can help you purchase some excellent cash flow vehicles like bridge loans or rental properties (using your cash value as collateral), but in and of itself whole life is not an efficient vehicle for cash flow.

Plus, as mentioned two lies ago, there are some types of money--IRA and qualified retirement plan money--that whole life can't accept. If you have either of those, they'll need to be invested elsewhere.

So you don't need to limit yourself to whole life and only whole life, and we wouldn't advise you to. Invest as much as you'd like in reliable vehicles for growth and/or cash flow. Just get your emergency/ opportunity fund set up first. (And if you'd like help with investments that fit the goals stated above, please feel free to reach out to us.)

Busting the Life Insurance Lies

Lie #29:
YOU CAN BORROW AGAINST YOUR POLICY AND NEVER PAY IT BACK

Here's another lie that's situationally true, but not generally recommended. As we saw two lies ago, it is possible to borrow against your policy and never repay it...if (and only if) you die before the loan interest has gotten too big. In that case, your death benefit repays the loan for you. So if you are 10-20 years from death, and you have been growing your policy since your 20s or 30s, this tactic can potentially work. But repeated borrowing builds up growing interest charges in the policy which can lead to the policy imploding. This means there is no more death benefit, and the policy owner could get hit with a large tax bill.

How do you know if you're 10-20 years from death? Well, you don't really, which is why insurance companies use what's called the Commissioner's Standard Ordinary Mortality table. This table applies whole life policies to certain ages and mortality rates to make actuarial decisions. In the past, the CSO Mortality table has used a 100-year timeline (called Life 100), but now that people are living much longer than they used to, they use a 121-year timeline (called Life 121).

When life insurance companies used the 1980 CSO table, the strategy of borrowing against your cash value, running up a big loan, and having it paid off by the death benefit worked. Now that most insur-

145   Kim D. H. Butler and Jack Burns

ance companies use the 2001 CSO table, all policies are stretched out further because instead of working on a 100 year time frame (as the 1980 table did) they are working on a 121 year timeframe (as the 2001 table does). So even if you personally don't live until age 121, your policy is built to sustain itself in case you do. This means, however, that borrowing on the hope that you'll die before you need to pay it back may backfire.

If you started your policy in your 50s or 60s, it's better to use your death benefit as a "permission slip" to spend other assets (visit www. ProsperityPeaks.com/permission for the report and video on how that works) and keep the cash value unleveraged until you've spent down other assets first.

Alternately, you could withdraw some of your cash value instead of borrowing against it--you'll reduce the death benefit and the value of the policy, and you won't be able to put that money back in later, but you also won't have to repay it like a loan, nor will it accumulate an interest charge. On the whole, if you know you can't pay back a policy loan, we've found the "borrow and let the death benefit pay back the loan" tactic not to be as effective, realistic, or sustainable as the "withdraw and pay some tax (on all dollars withdrawn above basis)" option.

Depending on your situation, if you're simply looking to turn your policy into cash you can use, you might even be able to find a family member or investor who would be interested in purchasing your policy. Most people don't realize this is an option, but life insurance policies have been sold since 1911 when the US Supreme Court ruled that permanent life insurance policies were a saleable asset, much like a deed of trust on a property. When policies are sold on the secondary market (often to corporate investors), they're called "life settlements," and they can create a real win-win for investors and elderly policyowners who may no longer need or want their policies.

As with anything where you are trying to analyze something years in the future, there is a lot of guesswork, especially knowing that all you have to work with is today's dividend scale. So do make sure you have a long term viewpoint and an experienced advisor when looking at any income generated from your policy.

Lie #30:
WHEN YOU BORROW AGAINST A POLICY, YOU PAY INTEREST TO YOURSELF

This, sadly, is a lie we've heard directly from life insurance advisors. In a roundabout way it could have some truth in it, but advisors need to explain very clearly how borrowing and repayment really work to make sure this one stays busted.

Here's the reality of the situation. A mutual insurance company, by law, shares all of its profits with its policyholders. Whole life policies (most often sold from mutual companies, though sometimes from stock companies) are typically "participating" policies, meaning the policy itself benefits from those profits in the form of dividends. So you could say that some of the interest costs you paid to the insurance company do end up in your policy, but it's nowhere near as simple as it sounds. Just saying "you pay interest to yourself" is misleading and confusing. It's like saying that if you pay state income tax that you're really "paying taxes to yourself," because you eventually benefit from those taxes, perhaps through new roads or other improvements. There's a grain of truth to it, but there's a big difference between paying tax (or interest) and earning it.

A loan borrowed *against* cash value, borrowed *from* an insurance company, works just like a CD-secured loan at a bank. There is collateral which grows or earns interest (the cash value or the CD) and there is a loan which has interest costs. These are two separate transactions and two separate accounts. Unfortunately, some insurance

Busting the Life Insurance Lies

148

companies combine them by issuing a "net cash value" statement which subtracts the loan from the cash value. We understand why: if you canceled the policy the next day, you would only get the "net" (gross cash value minus loan) back. But it would help us all understand things better if they showed two accounts, cash value and loan.

So to be clear: when you borrow against your cash value, you are borrowing from the insurance company. That insurance company will charge you interest for the use of their money. That same insurance company will provide dividends (assuming they are paying them) based on the full or "gross" cash value, just like a bank would charge you interest on the loan and pay you interest on your CD. The fact that some of the interest you pay in may make its way back to you in the form of those dividends is tangential to the borrowing process, and indeed to the policy itself.

Unfortunately, the impact of this lie is that some people (advisors as well as policyholders) take it literally. They believe that the policy loan interest they are paying somehow literally ends up in their cash value account, which can lead to misguided financial decisions. For instance, if you're actually "paying interest to yourself," why not pay the highest interest rate possible? Why not take as many loans as you can? Why bother comparing the pros and cons of a policy loan with other financing?

We believe you should make fully informed financial decisions, and to do so, you should consider the costs of a policy loan carefully. For instance, your policy may be the perfect place to get cash for a business equipment loan, a kitchen remodel, or a down payment on a house or car. But in the low-interest rate environment at the time of this writing, you can finance even a used car for as low as 1.99% interest, and owner-occupied mortgages aren't much higher, if you have good credit. Using your policy to finance your own home or car could double the interest you'll pay, and so you might want to be more strategic about when you borrow from your policy.

There are many stronger and clearer benefits to having and borrowing against a whole life policy, and we feel advisors would serve their clients (you!) by focusing on those instead.

Busting the Life Insurance Lies

Kim D. H. Butler and Jack Burns

Part 6:

ADVANCED AND TECHNICAL LIES FOR ADVISORS AND SAVVY CLIENTS

In this final section, we'll talk about some life insurance lies that come up in more specific situations than our narrative could fit in. These lies are pretty technical, often involving complex industry language, intricate inner workings of different kinds of policies, or specific situations that fewer people tend to encounter. While none of them had a good place in Stephen and Kara's story, and some of them may not apply to you, all of them will be helpful if you'd like to dig a little deeper into the life insurance world--or to refer back to later if you come across one of these lies yourself. For advisors reading this book, these lies will provide perspective on some more advanced concepts than we've touched on so far, and we hope they'll prove helpful for your continued professional learning.

Lie #31:

UNIVERSAL LIFE GIVES POLICYHOLDERS MORE FLEXIBILITY, HIGHER INTEREST, AND LESS COST

Universal Life (UL) is a type of permanent life insurance that was introduced in the 1980s. It was designed and marketed as more flexible and therefore more attractive than whole life. It came with more options for premiums, a more flexible death benefit, and a similar savings component. It also offered higher interest rates, in an effort to compete with banks which, at that time, offered higher rates than most insurance companies did. Most people with insurance in the 1980s had whole life policies and loved them, but UL was pushed toward the new generation as the next best thing in life insurance. Younger consumers were dazzled by the promises of UL, and policyholders flocked to them, sometimes switching from whole life to universal life as recommended by their advisor.

Unfortunately, the folks who got Universal Life policies during this time got a pretty rude awakening later on. Simply put, there was (and still is) no way that ULs could perform as advertised and give policyholders the same benefits as whole life.

The structure of a UL means your cash value can't be guaranteed. (UL has a guaranteed interest rate, but not a guaranteed cash value, which, as we've learned, are two different things.) And if you have little or no cash value (a common problem in ULs, as policies are often under-funded with lower premiums), a high interest rate to grow that value won't help you. By contrast, in a whole life policy, the cash value has a guaranteed dollar figure and a guaranteed increase that never goes down. Dividends are not guaranteed, but if they are paid, they become a part of this guaranteed cash value, which again is guaranteed to rise every year.

Additionally, the death benefit on Universal Life is not guaranteed unless an extra rider is added (at an extra cost, of course). As the policyholder ages, the internal cost of mortality keeps increasing because the cost of insurance inside the UL policy is based on annually-renewable term life insurance. This means that the cost of the life insurance itself keeps rising over time until it can start to drain the policy's cash value. And since your cash value isn't guaranteed, it can be tapped by the company to pay for the rising costs of policy benefits. You end up needing bigger premiums to keep the policy in force.

Imagine paying into a UL policy for decades, then all of the sudden you find out your premium is going to double or triple, or else you'll lose your life insurance! This cannot happen with whole life, which has a guaranteed premium.

UL policies are sold as "permanent" insurance, but we're not sure why. For one thing, they don't endow the way whole life policies do, where cash value equals death benefit after a certain amount of time. But more importantly, ULs can become prohibitively expensive to keep around. These increasing premiums have reared up to bite thousands of unsuspecting UL policyholders over the last 30+ years. Many have had to surrender their policies after being unable to keep up payments. Many more have watched their cash value decline so far that the policy can't support its own death benefit anymore. (This is called "imploding;" see Appendix F1 for an illustration of what an imploding UL policy looks like.) So many have even

Busting the Life Insurance Lies

felt forced out of their own policies. A recent New York Times article noted several former UL policy owners who had to walk away from five figures of premium payments, paid over decades, while their companies appear to have raised premiums largely to continue paying stockholders massive dividends. This is unconscionable. And even when there's no potential for foul play, calling any policy "permanent" when it can implode or become prohibitively expensive doesn't make sense to us.

There are numerous specialized types of Universal Life that have these kinds of problems as well as potential additional issues. Two prominent examples are Indexed Universal Life and Variable Universal Life. Indexed UL, (also called IUL) is sold as having the upside of the stock market without the downside. However, this can be misleading because there are still all the insurance costs, as well as the cost of the options on the index, which can cause the cash value to go negative. In a down market year, zero interest (or even 2% interest) less costs can equal cash value of less than zero. And even in a good market year, the upside is generally much less than the policyholder expected after costs, fees, and sometimes a less than 100% "participation rate."

Variable UL (VUL) is sold as having a variety of separately managed accounts like mutual funds as it makes an attempt to combine an insurance vehicle and an investment. We don't recommend this, either. Actually, we don't recommend mutual funds at all, we think there are much better ways to invest, but if you absolutely want to be in stocks or bonds, you'll be better off separating your insurance and savings vehicle from your investments. Especially if you are invested in the market, we don't think it makes sense to lose the benefit of non-correlated, steady growth that whole life can provide. There are numerous fees involved in VUL as well, along with the market risks, plus you are still dealing with all the problems above from UL.

The place where UL and IUL policies have succeeded best is in their marketing. Many people have been enticed away from whole life, the tried-and-true, time-tested model that has served families and paid dividends for over 150 years. And while newer policy structures offer many promises, whole life offers something even better: profits. Participating mutual whole life companies pay their policyholders dividends that represent the *profits* of the company, and we think that is hard to beat.

All things considered, whole life is still the leader of the pack when it comes to permanent life insurance. ULs may appear to give the policyholder more control and flexibility at first, but as time progresses, the problematic lack of guarantees in these policies come clearly into view. If a UL is heavily funded, it can come very close to performing like a whole life policy that has enough cash value to pay the rising mortality costs, but in our opinion that's settling for second best.

Lie #32:
DIRECT RECOGNITION IS BAD, NON-DIRECT RECOGNITION IS GOOD

Here's the thing about direct recognition vs. non-direct recognition. It's basically one more way to put insurance companies in conflict with each other for no good reason. In reality, they're fairly similar, and in the long run, they're both fine. But since they've become such a loud issue recently, here's how they're different and some thoughts on which one might be a better option.

Direct recognition is the newer approach out of the two. When a policy has direct recognition, it means that a policy owner's dividends can be adjusted when their cash value is collateralized-- that is, when they've taken out a policy loan against it. It is important to note that this adjustment can have a slightly positive or slightly negative effect on dividends paid. Recall that the pool of capital insurance companies use to supply policy loans is also their investment portfolio, which they invest to provide both capital growth for the company and dividends for participating policy owners. When a policy owner takes a loan out of that pool, the pool shrinks, lowering its value and therefore the amount of dividends it can produce. But since all policy owners receive those dividends, the upshot of this is that everyone gets a lower return because some policy owners have taken out loans. Eventually this tends to even out, but in the short run it isn't always fair.

Direct recognition solves this issue. Instead of having all policy-holders receive the same dividends across the board, it calculates dividends based on how much money a policy owner has taken out in loans. Those owners with large loans out will receive smaller dividends than those with no loans out. This is often pointed to as a negative, since some people are actually losing money on it--but remember, those people are also the ones who just received a significant amount of money in the form of their policy loans.

Non-direct recognition works the opposite way: everyone receives the same dividends no matter what. This was the only option available prior to the 1980s, before direct recognition was born. With non-direct recognition, dividends are not affected by outstanding policy loans. So it has the opposite tradeoff--owners with loans out don't take a larger hit on their dividends, but everyone takes a smaller hit on them in order to cover those loans being taken out in the first place, which means the company itself actually loses more in dividend value over time.

Again, everything tends to come out in the wash here, whether you have direct or non-direct recognition policies. And pointing fingers at one or the other as inherently bad doesn't really help anyone (and it tends to hurt the industry as a whole). But in the short and medium term, direct recognition does tend to be the more *fair* of the two, since it only lowers dividends for the people who have taken out loans. It also allows for longer-term stability for the insurance company itself, since their overall dividend value (and thus their portfolio return) will be higher. So if we had to recommend one over the other, we'd go with direct.

Ultimately, as a policyowner, you're fine either way. Both types of policies have a fan base, and there's no need to regret owning either type of policy. If you are concerned, just get one of each.

Busting the Life Insurance Lies

Lie #33:

YOU NEVER WANT TO PURCHASE A MEC, OR LET YOUR POLICY BECOME ONE

MEC stands for Modified Endowment Contract. Your policy transforms into a MEC when the cumulative premium payments surpasses a certain amount as determined by the Internal Revenue Service. MEC status is tested annually and also by a 7-pay test, which is a limit on how much you can put into your policy during the first seven years. The goal of the 7-pay test is to discourage payments that would cause a paid-up policy within the first seven years.

If you purchase a policy that is a MEC, such as a single-premium policy, or if your whole life policy becomes a MEC, any money taken out of it or borrowed against it will be subject to income tax and sometimes additional penalties. And once a policy becomes a MEC, it can't ever be changed back, though it doesn't affect the income-tax-free nature of the death benefit.

Even if your policy is past the seven-year mark, you'll still want to be very careful with how much you're paying into it. For one thing, policies are tested for MEC status annually and every seven years, so you aren't out of the woods just because you've had the policy for over seven years. Also, a policy can still become a MEC even if it survives the initial 7-pay test due to extra Paid-Up Additions.

With all that being said, there are some limited occasions when MECs can work well. If you have a large lump sum of money you want to put into a life insurance policy, rather than making payments over 7+ years, a MEC can make sense, especially if your focus is more on the death benefit. Also, if you don't plan on using your cash value for any loans or withdrawals (or if you have a different policy you can use for loans), the potential of taking a tax hit on those loans or withdrawals won't matter--and if you do end up needing to withdraw or take a loan, if you're over 59½, you'll only have to pay taxes on those amounts, no other penalties. (In this way, a MEC acts like a non-qualified retirement plan.)

Finally, MECs work really well for estate transfer--in fact, that's what they were initially designed for. If your main goal in taking out the life insurance policy is to pass along cash to another generation via the death benefit, using a MEC allows you to maximize that cash without worrying about being penalized for growing or compiling it too quickly.

It's worth noting here that it's hard to turn your whole life policy into a MEC by accident, as the insurance companies alert you if you have put more money into your policy than would be allowed by the MEC limits. Your company can even rescind a transaction that would cause your policy to to become a MEC. If you do overpay by accident, you have 60 days to make adjustments accordingly. So you don't need to be too scared about inadvertently stumbling into a MEC--just be aware of what it takes to do so, and always open your mail from the insurance company!

While MECs aren't usually ideal for a typical policy owner (remember that Evan warned Kara and Stephen against paying so much that their policy turned into one), there are definitely situations where they can be beneficial. (See Appendix C4).

(For more information about MECs, there is an excellent article on RetirementThinkTank.com called "The Truth About Modified Endowment Contracts.")

Busting the Life Insurance Lies

Lie #34:

ON A LIFE INSURANCE LOAN, YOU CAN PAY THE INTEREST IN ADVANCE OR IN ARREARS

This lie is largely due to confusion around how interest is described, not how it's actually paid. Interest on a life insurance loan is *always* charged and paid in advance, either by the policy owner writing a check, or by the insurance company deducting it from the policy's cash value or adding it to the loan amount.

But there are two different ways to talk about that interest: in advance or in arrears. And some advisors have been known to mistakenly offer paying interest in advance as a benefit that saves the policyholder money by giving a lower interest rate, which it doesn't actually do. What it really means is that if you pay in advance, you borrow slightly less money, since you don't have to borrow the interest itself--you've already paid it, up front.

Had you paid the interest in arrears (that is, after paying back the rest of the loan), you'd still have paid the same interest rate. You simply would have borrowed a bit more in the first place to cover that interest, and thus have a bit more to pay back. Either way, the interest rate on the loan would be exactly the same.

So the bad news (and the lie) is that you don't really have a choice here: you'll always pay interest in advance. The good news, though, is that by doing so you'll borrow a little less, and thus pay back a little less, than you might have otherwise.

Lie #35:

ON A LIFE INSURANCE LOAN, YOU CAN CHOOSE BETWEEN SIMPLE AND COMPOUND INTEREST

This is another lie that arises from confusing statements advisors sometimes make. In this case, it's about how policy owners repay their loans, and how to do so most advantageously.

A quick review of terms to start: simple interest is interest that only applies to the principal of the loan. If you take out $10,000 at 12%, you'll only ever pay that 12% interest on the $10,000 principal, which would total $1,200. Compound interest recalculates the principal periodically based on how much interest has accrued on it, and then charges the interest amount on that new principal every time. So let's say that 12% interest on your $10,000 loan is compounded monthly. The first month your interest would be 1% of $10,000, which is $100. Then if no payments were made, the second month it would be 1% of the sum of those two amounts, $10,100, which would raise your monthly interest charge to $102. The third month would raise the monthly interest to $103 and so on.

Here's where the lie comes into this: all policy loans have compound interest. So saying that there's a choice between the two interest types for your policy loan is incorrect. More importantly, not understanding how compound interest will affect repaying that loan will cost you. Because policy loan interest is compounded, if you pay the

Busting the Life Insurance Lies

162

ing and raising the amount of the loan. In other words, the less consistent you are about paying your loans back, the more you'll have to pay on them over time.

So don't let the interest on policy loans creep up on you and drain your funds! Make a plan to pay the loans back in a timely fashion, and if you cannot do so, talk with your advisor and see if it makes more sense to do a withdrawal to pay back the policy loan all at once. (Yes, it's possible to "pay off" a previous loan with a withdrawal, if you find you can't successfully pay it back out of your current cash flow.)

Lie #36:
YOU NEED BUY-SELL INSURANCE TO PROTECT YOUR BUSINESS

If you are a business owner or an aspiring business owner, you've probably been advised to get buy-sell insurance. Buy-sell agreements determine when owners in a company can sell their interest, who can buy that interest, and at what price, and are supported by insurance policies taken out by business partners on each other. (Triggering events for buy-sell agreements typically include death, disability, bankruptcy, and a few other similar possibilities.)

Of course, you want to have some sort of policy in place to protect your business and those who would inherit your business if something happened to you, right? Buy-sell insurance is commonly sold as the insurance that will do that, and in many cases it can. But here's the thing about buy-sell insurance: it creates a policy on you that you don't own. Either your business partner owns it, or the company itself does.

Now, the buy-sell agreement provides for this by having you take out a policy on your business partner concurrently to their taking one out on you. So if you die, and your partner doesn't want to work with your spouse, they can use the death benefit they receive from that policy to buy out the rest of the company. If your partner dies first, you can do the same thing. Alternately, if you don't have a partner or would rather do it differently, you can have the business itself be

Busting the Life Insurance Lies

164

your policy's beneficiary, so if you die the business will have a better chance to stay afloat after you're gone.

In theory, all of that sounds great. But in practice, it doesn't always work. For one thing, if the business is failing and one of its assets is a substantial life insurance policy on one or more of its owners, the cash value of those policies is one of the first things bankruptcy creditors will raid. For another, what if the business has grown in value, and the agreed-upon buyout is much lower than your share of the business is currently worth? Or on the other hand, what if the business has tanked, but you still have to pay your partner's family what it was worth when it was solvent? Your family is suddenly out all of that money.

The underlying issue here is that when a buy-sell agreement is set up, it's based on a business's current value *at the time of agreement*. The policies supporting that agreement can't typically change enough in value to follow the business's growth or decline over time. And since you don't have a crystal ball, there's no way to know when a partner will die, or how much the business will be worth at that time. So owners with buy-sell agreements funded with life insurance can never fund their policies at the right amount, and ultimately, neither party gets their money's worth--either the death benefit is greater than the business's value, or vice versa. So what starts out seeming fair and equitable can fall out of proportion over time.

We'd like to suggest this alternative: get life insurance that you can control. Don't set up an insurance policy that doesn't directly benefit you and your family. With a personally owned whole life policy that designates your family as the beneficiary, you can make sure your death benefit goes to them immediately, without any questions or negotiations. Additionally, you may choose to buy a second policy where your business or your partner is the beneficiary. But we don't recommend doing that until and unless you already have personal insurance for your family.

Lie #37:

YOU NEED KEY PERSON INSURANCE ON IMPORTANT EMPLOYEES BUT DON'T NEED YOUR OWN INSURANCE

Imagine a five-star restaurant losing its executive chef without warning. A hospital whose chief of surgery suddenly passes on. A construction company whose head project manager has an accident. A nonprofit whose executive director becomes fatally ill.

Suddenly these businesses are in serious trouble. Not only do they have to scramble to maintain the status quo without their most important employee, but they have to find, onboard, and train a replacement, stat. In almost every situation like this, the company loses momentum, which means they also lose money. Sometimes they never recover.

Obviously the personal impact, knowledge, and leadership of a crucial employee are irreplaceable. But the financial security they bring to a company is not. This is why many businesses now take out "key person" life insurance policies on their executives, policies where if the recipient dies, the company receives a death benefit. This type of policy gives the business an emergency cushion of funds to help them through the months of potentially lean times following the sudden death of a key person.

Having a policy like this in place can make the difference between solvency and bankruptcy, between having the time to ensure survival and going under. If you own a business and you have an employee whose death would make everything in your company grind to a halt, you absolutely should consider taking out a key person policy on them.

What's so surprising here is how many executives and other high-level employees allow their businesses to take out key person policies on them--but never take out any policies for themselves! This strikes us as backwards. Why would you let a policy be taken out on you that would benefit everyone *but* your family? Or why would you get policies for other people but not protect yourself? If the only person or entity who benefits after you pass is the business that employs you, you might want to reexamine your priorities.

It's always possible for a person to have more than one policy on themselves, as long as the policies don't equal more than that person's total Human Life Value. So if your company wants to take out a key person policy on you, great, but you might want to make sure at least some of that HLV will go to your family first. And if you can only have one policy, make it your own, not your employer's.

Busting the Life Insurance Lies

Lie #38:
THE "GROSS DIVIDEND" RATE EQUALS WHAT YOU'LL RECEIVE IN DIVIDENDS

If you find an interest rate on an insurance company's website when they are talking about dividends, they're referring to *gross* dividends: the dividend amount before expenses. Expenses include the cost of the death benefit, the advisor's commission, and the administrative cost of running the mutual company, and they come out of dividend returns before the dividends are passed on to you. Typically after those costs are removed, you'll see around a 3.5%-5% "net dividend" during the year 2016.

This net dividend number also gets confused with the stated 4% guaranteed interest rate, which is actually a guaranteed dollar figure if no dividends are paid. Assuming no dividends are ever paid, that effective 4% is also a gross interest rate with the same costs above (death benefit, commission, and administration expenses) taken from it, to net down to 2 or 2.5%.

Please remember, one of the most important things about whole life is that once a dividend is paid and reinvested, it becomes a part of that guaranteed cash value, never to go down again unless you borrow against it so much that you implode your policy as mentioned earlier. More importantly here, please also remember that "gross" means "before expenses" and "net" means "after expenses." So if you see a "gross dividend" rate, know that it will be subject to expenses before it gets to you.

We find that many advisors do not understand the difference between gross dividend rates and net internal rate of return earned on cash value. (See Appendix G.) Be sure to find and work with an advisor who knows the difference between net and gross, and can explain to you how that is calculated.

Kim D. H. Butler and Jack Burns

Conclusion

Finding the time, energy, and motivation to take control of your personal financial situation isn't easy. It can feel so much simpler to find an investment advisor to handle it for you, or to sock money away in a savings account or 401(k), or even not to think about your finances at all, hoping that somehow everything will work out. And once most people have opted to do one of those things, they rarely give it a second thought...until it's too late.

Jack's dad had a saying that really applies here: "Sometimes in life, we're only entitled to one mistake." You don't want that mistake to be finding out you aren't getting what you wanted (or what you thought you were getting) from your life insurance, your other assets, or your financial situation in general. It just makes no sense to work so hard for so many years, and end up with less than what you could have and should have. But far too many people do exactly that.

Clearly, one reason for that is the presence of all the lies we've talked about in this book so far. Whether you run into common general lies or a complicated technical lie, there's a lot of confusing information out there, and we hope our words here will help you navigate those treacherous waters with success. But there's one more lie we haven't addressed in so many words: the lie that says *you have to figure all of this out for yourself.* This lie might be the most insidious of all, because more than any other it tends to stop people from looking into life insurance before they even start.

Under the spell of this lie, people think things like: it's too complicated, it'll never make sense, it's like another language, I don't have time to learn a whole new industry, I don't know who to ask for help, I'll just forget it. Financial advisors have capitalized on this confusion by selling themselves as compassionate guides to financial security, and their investment vehicles as easy, simple, basic, no-thought-required paths to reliable financial success--while painting life insurance advisors as greedy gremlins who use complex jargon to walk away with more of your money.

We hope you get by now how far that picture is from the truth. Yes, life insurance takes a bit of work to understand, and trying to master and implement it alone can be daunting--even we wouldn't do that, and we've spent years studying it. But that's why it's a lie: you don't have to go alone. Most life insurance advisors are like Evan Holmes and Carl Parsons. They want to help you understand their industry's offerings, so you can find and implement the policies that will get you the most money and security in the long run--money you can use now and later, and security for your life *and* your heirs.

So if you're a potential policy owner, don't be afraid of the Big Bad Insurance Advisor. Even if they do have big eyes, ears, or noses, they'll use them to help you find the right policies for you and your family. (The big teeth they save for stockbrokers.) And if you're an advisor reading this, consider sharing this book with your clients as well as keeping it as a resource for your own work. Handing a potential client a book called *Busting the Life Insurance Lies* could go a long way toward assuring them that you're working in their best interest.

Thank you for reading! We hope you, like our illustrative couple Stephen and Kara, feel more confident and purposeful about life insurance now. If you're wondering where to go from here, know that there are many great advisors out there who want to work with you, not just for you--including us! Our favorite part of this work is forming beautiful partnerships with our clients that last many, many years. We can both work nationwide by phone or online, so if you would like more information, have any questions, or would like to schedule a get-to-know-you call, please reach out to Kim at kim@partners4prosperity.com or Jack at jack@jblife.com. We would love to connect with you!

Kim D. H. Butler and Jack Burns

Appendices

Life Insurance Illustrations

Based on the 2016 Dividend Scale

EXPLANATION OF TERMS AND COLUMN DESCRIPTIONS:

Please remember these illustrations are proportional, meaning you can double it or cut it in half and all the numbers for premiums, paid up additions, cash value, and death benefit will adjust proportionally.

Additional Riders are also available, such as Waiver of Premium and Guaranteed Insurability Option (GIO).

Dividend Option: Paid-Up Additions. Dividends in this illustration have been elected to automatically go towards Paid-Up Additions, adding to Cash Value while also increasing Death Benefit. You also have other dividend options such as using dividends to pay down policy loans, or receiving dividends as income, which many of our clients do in their later years.

Below the line:

Guaranteed Section: Guarantees include level premiums, minimum death benefit (assuming premiums are paid), and a base level of guaranteed cash value. The guaranteed cash value is a dollar figure (not an interest rate).

Busting the Life Insurance Lies

Non-Guaranteed Section: These figures include dividends and optional (unscheduled) Paid-Up Additions. We can usually count on these figures even though they are not guaranteed because once a dividend gets paid it becomes part of the guaranteed cash value and most good mutual insurance companies have paid a dividend every year for over 100 years.

Column Descriptions:

Policy Year, Age at Start of Year: Self-explanatory. Note some companies list Age at End of Year and others round up so if you are 45 1/2, they'll consider you insurance age 46.

Base Policy Annual Premium - This would be the minimal amount to keep policy in force, and includes no PUAs. Note that the bulk of premiums are added to Guaranteed Cash Value after the first year, similar to Paid-Up Additions and Dividends.

Base Guaranteed Cash Value is a guaranteed dollar figure, not an interest rate. This is the "base" guaranteed figure if you paid ONLY the base policy premium and added no Paid-Up Additions or Dividends.

Annual Dividends - projected, not guaranteed. These Life Insurance Illustrations are based on 2016 dividend scale. The amount varies year-to-year and is announced prior to the previous year's end. Most mutual insurance companies have paid a dividend every year for well over 100 years. Though not guaranteed, dividends are extremely reliable historically.

The Cash Value of All Additions is ONLY the cash value from the PUAs. This assumed the maximum amount of unscheduled PUAs have been contributed.

The Net Cash Value column is your TOTAL cash value. This is your CLUE account (Control, Liquidity, Use and Equity) that you can borrow against. Remember, it is borrowing against, not from.

Death Benefit - notice it is increasing annually, due to PUAs and Dividends being added to the policy. It must do this so the policy does not become a MEC.

Additional Notes: Regardless of which insurance company you are looking at, these columns will be similar. Remember, there are no "deals" in the life insurance industry! Life insurance (and the whole life product) have been around too long for one company to do better than another one consistently over time. If there appear to be differences, they are short lived and a few years later, another company will rise to what appears to be the top for a few years. Long term, all the top mutual life insurance companies are nearly the same. What matters most is not which company you use, but what you DO with the policy yourself. Specifically, the critical strategies are to fund it as long as you can, utilize your cash value to get your dollars working harder, and pay back all loans over time.

Kim D. H. Butler and Jack Burns

ILLUSTRATION APPENDICES TABLE OF CONTENTS

Illustration	Age	Lies	Page
A1 - Max PUA	10	4, 10, 22, 24	182
A2 - No PUA	10	4, 10, 22, 24	184
B1 - Fullpay + Max PUA	35	4, 14, 17, 18, 22, 23, 24	186
B2 - Max PUA, Natural Vanish	35	4, 14, 17, 18, 22, 23, 24	188
B3 - No PUA	35	4, 14, 17, 18, 22, 23, 24	190
B4 - 1-4 Yearly Renewable Term	35	4, 14, 17, 18, 22, 23, 24	192
B5 - 30 Year Level Term	35	4, 14, 17, 18, 22, 23, 24	200
C1 - Full Pay Partial PUA	50	4, 18, 22, 23, 33	202
C2 - Max PUA, Natural Vanish	50	4, 18, 22, 23, 33	204
C3 - No PUA	50	4, 18, 22, 23, 33	206
C4 - MEC	50	4, 18, 22, 23, 33	208
D1 - Death Benefit, Partial PUA	75	4, 11, 17, 22, 23, 24	210
D2 - Max PUA	75	4, 11, 17, 22, 23, 24	212
D3 - No PUA	75	4, 11, 17, 22, 23, 24	214

Illustration	Age	Lies	Page
E1 - Inforce Full Pay Male	47	19	216
E2 - Half Death Benefit Sample	47	19	220
E3 - Reduced Paid Up	47	19	222
F1 - UL "Dying on the Vine"	47	31	224
F2 - UL "Dying on the Vine"	28	31	226
G - Whole Truth Funding with Kim Butler and Todd Langford	35	1, 15, 26, 28	228

APPENDIX A1

MAX PUA - MALE, AGE 10
Whole Life 95 Illustration

		Guaranteed		
POL YR	AGE AT START OF YEAR	BASE POLICY ANNUAL PREM #	BASE GUAR. CASH VALUE ##	END OF YEAR DIVIDEND ## *
1	10	753	19	0
2	11	753	603	127
3	12	753	1,013	136
4	13	753	1,433	99
5	14	753	1,862	109
6	15	753	2,295	123
7	16	753	2,732	141
8	17	753	3,175	160
9	18	753	3,628	177
10	19	753	4,096	195
11	20	753	4,559	213
12	21	753	5,040	228
13	22	753	5,539	249
14	23	753	6,058	269
15	24	753	6,596	290
106	115	0	100,000	94,673
107	116	0	100,000	99,454
108	117	0	100,000	104,477
109	118	0	100,000	109,753
110	119	0	100,000	115,295
111	120	0	100,000	121,118

Concept Based on the 2016 Dividend Scale

Non-Guaranteed

NET AFTER TAX OUTLAY # *	CUM NET A/T OUTLAY # *	CASH VALUE OF ALL ADDS ## *	NET CASH VALUE ## *	NET DEATH BENEFIT ## *
1,568	1,568	803	822	108,591
1,568	3,136	1,764	2,367	116,998
1,568	4,704	2,768	3,781	126,302
1,568	6,272	3,770	5,203	135,315
1,568	7,840	4,816	6,678	143,701
1,568	9,408	5,908	8,203	151,892
1,568	10,976	7,052	9,784	159,939
1,568	12,544	8,246	11,421	167,882
1,568	14,112	9,494	13,122	175,727
1,568	15,680	10,801	14,897	183,456
1,568	17,248	12,170	16,729	191,081
1,568	18,816	13,604	18,644	198,597
1,568	20,384	15,107	20,646	205,991
1,568	21,952	16,683	22,741	213,292
1,436	23,388	18,207	24,803	219,631
0	98,998	1,870,380	1,970,380	1,970,380
0	98,998	1,969,834	2,069,834	2,069,834
0	98,998	2,074,311	2,174,311	2,174,311
0	98,998	2,184,064	2,284,064	2,284,064
0	98,998	2,299,359	2,399,359	2,399,359
0	98,998	2,420,477	2,520,477	2,520,477

APPENDIX A2
NO PUA - MALE, AGE 10
Whole Life 95 Illustration

			Guaranteed	
POL YR	AGE AT START OF YEAR	BASE POLICY ANNUAL PREM #	BASE GUAR. CASH VALUE ##	END OF YEAR DIVIDEND ## *
1	10	753	19	0
2	11	753	603	121
3	12	753	1,013	126
4	13	753	1,433	83
5	14	753	1,862	88
6	15	753	2,295	95
7	16	753	2,732	105
8	17	753	3,175	115
9	18	753	3,628	122
10	19	753	4,096	131
11	20	753	4,559	138
12	21	753	5,040	144
13	22	753	5,539	153
14	23	753	6,058	161
15	24	753	6,596	170
31	40	753	18,608	525
32	41	753	19,601	550
33	42	753	20,621	577
34	43	753	21,669	607
35	44	753	22,742	640

Busting the Life Insurance Lies

Concept Based on the 2016 Dividend Scale

Non-Guaranteed

NET AFTER TAX OUTLAY # *	CUM NET A/T OUTLAY # *	CASH VALUE OF ALL ADDS ## *	NET CASH VALUE ## *	NET DEATH BENEFIT ## *
753	753	0	19	100,000
753	1,506	121	724	100,121
753	2,259	251	1,264	101,373
753	3,012	343	1,776	102,579
753	3,765	443	2,305	103,381
753	4,518	554	2,849	104,201
753	5,271	678	3,410	105,064
753	6,024	816	3,991	105,985
753	6,777	965	4,593	106,958
753	7,530	1,128	5,224	107,959
753	8,283	1,303	5,862	108,992
753	9,036	1,491	6,531	110,047
753	9,789	1,694	7,233	111,118
753	10,542	1,912	7,970	112,215
753	11,295	2,146	8,742	113,332
753	23,343	11,343	29,951	142,228
753	24,096	12,287	31,888	144,276
753	24,849	13,289	33,910	146,351
753	25,602	14,353	36,022	148,459
753	26,355	15,480	38,222	150,606

Appendix B1

FULL PAY PLUS MAX PUA - MALE, AGE 35
Whole Life 95 Illustration

POL YR	AGE AT START OF YEAR	Guaranteed		END OF YEAR DIVIDEND ## *
		BASE POLICY ANNUAL PREM #	BASE GUAR. CASH VALUE ##	
1	35	1,510	52	0
2	36	1,510	1,362	170
3	37	1,510	2,458	197
4	38	1,510	3,590	178
5	39	1,510	4,759	209
6	40	1,510	5,966	244
7	41	1,510	7,210	280
8	42	1,510	8,489	319
9	43	1,510	9,805	365
10	44	1,510	11,155	413
11	45	1,510	12,404	463
12	46	1,510	13,683	516
13	47	1,510	14,994	570
14	48	1,510	16,348	618
15	49	1,510	17,745	708
81	115	0	100,000	55,487
82	116	0	100,000	58,289
83	117	0	100,000	61,232
84	118	0	100,000	64,325
85	119	0	100,000	67,573
86	120	0	100,000	70,985

Busting the Life Insurance Lies

Concept Based on the 2016 Dividend Scale

Non-Guaranteed

NET AFTER TAX OUTLAY # *	CUM NET A/T OUTLAY # *	CASH VALUE OF ALL ADDS ## *	NET CASH VALUE ## *	NET DEATH BENEFIT ## *
2,542	2,542	1,015	1,067	104,652
2,542	5,084	2,236	3,598	109,315
2,542	7,626	3,527	5,985	114,434
2,542	10,168	4,844	8,434	119,448
2,542	12,710	6,237	10,996	124,262
2,542	15,251	7,714	13,680	129,040
2,542	17,793	9,277	16,487	133,795
2,542	20,335	10,931	19,420	138,530
2,542	22,877	12,685	22,490	143,255
2,542	25,419	14,543	25,698	147,987
2,542	27,961	16,508	28,912	152,728
2,542	30,503	18,587	32,270	157,480
2,542	33,045	20,785	35,779	162,250
2,542	35,587	23,103	39,451	167,029
2,542	38,129	25,587	43,332	171,839
0	117,869	1,055,222	1,155,222	1,155,222
0	117,869	1,113,511	1,213,511	1,213,511
0	117,869	1,174,743	1,274,743	1,274,743
0	117,869	1,239,068	1,339,068	1,339,068
0	117,869	1,306,641	1,406,641	1,406,641
0	117,869	1,377,626	1,477,626	1,477,626

Appendix B2

MAX PUA'S WITH NATURAL VANISH – MALE, AGE 35

Whole Life 95 Illustration

		Guaranteed		
POL YR	AGE AT START OF YEAR	BASE POLICY ANNUAL PREM #	BASE GUAR. CASH VALUE ##	END OF YEAR DIVIDEND ## *
1	35	1,510	52	0
2	36	1,510	1,362	193
3	37	1,510	2,458	232
4	38	1,510	3,590	227
5	39	1,510	4,759	273
6	40	1,510	5,966	324
7	41	1,510	7,210	377
8	42	1,510	8,489	395
9	43	1,510	9,805	418
10	44	1,510	11,155	440
11	45	1,510	12,404	462
12	46	1,510	13,683	484
13	47	1,510	14,994	506
14	48	1,510	16,348	519
15	49	1,510	17,745	572
66	100	0	100,000	8,213
67	101	0	100,000	8,627
68	102	0	100,000	9,063
69	103	0	100,000	9,521
70	104	0	100,000	10,002

Busting the Life Insurance Lies

Based on the 2016 Dividend Scale

Non-Guaranteed

NET AFTER TAX OUTLAY # *	CUM NET A/T OUTLAY # *	CASH VALUE OF ALL ADDS ## *	NET CASH VALUE ## *	NET DEATH BENEFIT ## *
3,708	3,708	2,162	2,214	109,908
3,708	7,416	4,593	5,955	119,671
3,708	11,124	7,150	9,608	129,807
3,708	14,832	9,790	13,380	139,723
3,708	18,540	12,568	17,327	149,330
3,708	22,248	15,493	21,459	158,800
3,708	25,956	18,570	25,780	168,152
0	25,956	18,040	26,529	163,932
0	25,956	17,510	27,315	159,921
0	25,956	16,979	28,134	156,124
0	25,956	16,446	28,850	152,527
0	25,956	15,913	29,596	149,118
0	25,956	15,380	30,374	145,891
0	25,956	14,843	31,191	142,825
0	25,956	14,341	32,086	139,938
0	25,956	71,830	171,830	171,830
0	25,956	80,458	180,458	180,458
0	25,956	89,521	189,521	189,521
0	25,956	99,042	199,042	199,042
0	25,956	109,043	209,043	209,043

* Natural vanish / offset

Appendix B3
NO PUA - MALE, AGE 35
Whole Life 95 Illustration

		Guaranteed		
POL YR	AGE AT START OF YEAR	BASE POLICY ANNUAL PREM #	BASE GUAR. CASH VALUE ##	END OF YEAR DIVIDEND ## *
1	35	1,510	52	0
2	36	1,510	1,362	150
3	37	1,510	2,458	166
4	38	1,510	3,590	134
5	39	1,510	4,759	152
6	40	1,510	5,966	173
7	41	1,510	7,210	194
8	42	1,510	8,489	217
9	43	1,510	9,805	244
10	44	1,510	11,155	272
11	45	1,510	12,404	300
12	46	1,510	13,683	330
13	47	1,510	14,994	360
14	48	1,510	16,348	385
15	49	1,510	17,745	450
81	115	0	100,000	32,445
82	116	0	100,000	34,083
83	117	0	100,000	35,805
84	118	0	100,000	37,613
85	119	0	100,000	39,512
86	120	0	100,000	41,507

Busting the Life Insurance Lies

Concept Based on the 2016 Dividend Scale

Non-Guaranteed

NET AFTER TAX OUTLAY # *	CUM NET A/T OUTLAY # *	CASH VALUE OF ALL ADDS ## *	NET CASH VALUE ## *	NET DEATH BENEFIT ## *
1,510	1,510	0	52	100,000
1,510	3,020	150	1,512	100,150
1,510	4,530	321	2,779	100,830
1,510	6,040	466	4,056	101,506
1,510	7,550	635	5,394	102,078
1,510	9,060	830	6,796	102,706
1,510	10,570	1,053	8,263	103,393
1,510	12,080	1,306	9,795	104,139
1,510	13,590	1,595	11,400	104,946
1,510	15,100	1,921	13,076	105,823
1,510	16,610	2,285	14,689	106,766
1,510	18,120	2,691	16,374	107,773
1,510	19,630	3,141	18,135	108,844
1,510	21,140	3,630	19,978	109,968
1,510	22,650	4,200	21,945	111,171
0	90,600	575,908	675,908	675,908
0	90,600	609,991	709,991	709,991
0	90,600	645,795	745,795	745,795
0	90,600	683,408	783,408	783,408
0	90,600	722,920	822,920	822,920
0	90,600	764,428	864,428	864,428

Kim D. H. Butler and Jack Burns

Appendix B4-1

YEARLY RENEWABLE TERM

Male, Age 35

POL YR	AGE AT START OF YEAR	Non-Guaranteed - Current	
		SCHED. NET PREMIUM #*	ACCUM SCHED. PREMIUM #*
1	35	248	248
2	36	255	503
3	37	265	768
4	38	275	1,043
5	39	293	1,335
6	40	310	1,645
7	41	328	1,973
8	42	345	2,318
9	43	363	2,680
10	44	385	3,065
11	45	420	3,485
12	46	458	3,943
13	47	495	4,438
14	48	535	4,973
15	49	570	5,543
16	50	610	6,153
17	51	658	6,810
18	52	713	7,523
19	53	775	8,298
20	54	853	9,150
21	55	935	10,085
22	56	1,020	11,105
23	57	1,118	12,223
24	58	1,215	13,438
25	59	1,323	14,760

Busting the Life Insurance Lies

Guaranteed

MAXIMUM NET PREMIUM #	ACCUM. MAX/NET PREMIUM #	DEATH BENEFIT ##*
248	248	250,000
420	668	250,000
435	1,103	250,000
463	1,565	250,000
488	2,053	250,000
518	2,570	250,000
555	3,125	250,000
600	3,725	250,000
655	4,380	250,000
718	5,098	250,000
788	5,885	250,000
858	6,743	250,000
933	7,675	250,000
975	8,650	250,000
1,025	9,675	250,000
1,098	10,773	250,000
1,183	11,955	250,000
1,298	13,253	250,000
1,423	14,675	250,000
1,583	16,258	250,000
1,780	18,038	250,000
1,980	20,018	250,000
2,195	22,213	250,000
2,380	24,593	250,000
2,593	27,185	250,000

Appendix B4-2
YEARLY RENEWABLE TERM (CONTINUED)
Male, Age 35

		Non-Guaranteed - Current	
POL YR	AGE AT START OF YEAR	SCHED. NET PREMIUM #*	ACCUM SCHED. PREMIUM #*
26	60	1,438	16,198
27	61	1,575	17,773
28	62	1,730	19,503
29	63	1,913	21,415
30	64	2,118	23,533
31	65	2,348	25,880
32	66	2,610	28,490
33	67	2,893	31,383
34	68	3,210	34,593
35	69	3,540	38,133
36	70	3,885	42,018
37	71	4,325	46,343
38	72	4,815	51,158
39	73	5,363	56,520
40	74	5,973	62,493
41	75	6,653	69,145
42	76	7,410	76,555
43	77	8,255	84,810
44	78	9,198	94,008
45	79	10,248	104,255
46	80	11,420	115,675
47	81	12,750	128,425
48	82	14,123	142,548
49	83	15,595	158,143
50	84	17,220	175,363

Busting the Life Insurance Lies

Guaranteed

MAXIMUM NET PREMIUM #	ACCUM. MAX/NET PREMIUM #	DEATH BENEFIT ##*
2,848	30,033	250,000
3,160	33,193	250,000
3,543	36,735	250,000
3,970	40,705	250,000
4,420	45,125	250,000
4,895	50,020	250,000
5,375	55,395	250,000
5,863	61,258	250,000
6,388	67,645	250,000
6,933	74,578	250,000
7,593	82,170	250,000
8,330	90,500	250,000
9,298	99,798	250,000
10,320	110,118	250,000
11,395	121,513	250,000
12,570	134,083	250,000
13,850	147,933	250,000
15,338	163,270	250,000
17,075	180,345	250,000
19,083	199,428	250,000
21,270	220,698	250,000
23,760	244,458	250,000
26,355	270,813	250,000
29,150	299,963	250,000
32,248	332,210	250,000

Appendix B4-3
YEARLY RENEWABLE TERM (CONTINUED)
Male, Age 35

POL YR	AGE AT START OF YEAR	Non-Guaranteed - Current	
		SCHED. NET PREMIUM #*	ACCUM SCHED. PREMIUM #*
51	85	19,033	194,395
52	86	21,520	215,915
53	87	24,283	240,198
54	88	27,300	267,498
55	89	30,555	298,053
56	90	34,023	332,075
57	91	37,385	369,460
58	92	40,950	410,410
59	93	44,768	455,178
60	94	48,858	504,035
61	95	53,213	557,248
62	96	57,313	614,560
63	97	61,710	676,270
64	98	66,425	742,695
65	99	71,483	814,178
66	100	76,900	891,078
67	101	82,708	973,785
68	102	88,933	1,062,718
69	103	95,595	1,158,313
70	104	102,735	1,261,048
71	105	110,300	1,371,348
72	106	118,400	1,489,748
73	107	127,073	1,616,820
74	108	136,348	1,753,168
75	109	146,280	1,899,448

Busting the Life Insurance Lies

Guaranteed

MAXIMUM NET PREMIUM #	ACCUM. MAX/NET PREMIUM #	DEATH BENEFIT ##*
35,708	367,918	250,000
39,543	407,460	250,000
43,730	451,190	250,000
48,218	499,408	250,000
52,950	552,358	250,000
57,893	610,250	250,000
62,538	672,788	250,000
67,383	740,170	250,000
72,493	812,663	250,000
77,888	890,550	250,000
83,558	974,108	250,000
88,745	1,062,853	250,000
94,275	1,157,128	250,000
100,180	1,257,308	250,000
106,480	1,363,788	250,000
113,218	1,477,005	250,000
118,563	1,595,568	250,000
124,260	1,719,828	250,000
130,323	1,850,150	250,000
136,773	1,986,923	250,000
143,538	2,130,460	250,000
150,733	2,281,193	250,000
158,380	2,439,573	250,000
166,508	2,606,080	250,000
175,143	2,781,223	250,000

Appendix B4-4

YEARLY RENEWABLE TERM (CONTINUED)

Male, Age 35

POL YR	AGE AT START OF YEAR	Non-Guaranteed - Current	
		SCHED. NET PREMIUM #*	ACCUM SCHED. PREMIUM #*
76	110	156,895	2,056,343
77	111	168,255	2,224,598
78	112	180,405	2,405,003
79	113	193,398	2,598,400
80	114	207,288	2,805,688
81	115	213,260	3,018,948

Busting the Life Insurance Lies

	Guaranteed	
MAXIMUM NET PREMIUM #	ACCUM. MAX/NET PREMIUM #	DEATH BENEFIT ##*
184,308	2,965,530	250,000
194,043	3,159,573	250,000
204,373	3,363,945	250,000
215,345	3,579,290	250,000
226,983	3,806,273	250,000
239,333	4,045,605	250,000

APPENDIX B5

LEVEL 30 YEAR TERM - MALE, AGE 35

POLICY YEAR	AGE AT START OF YEAR	ANNUAL PREMIUM #
1	35	468
2	36	468
3	37	468
4	38	468
5	39	468
6	40	468
7	41	468
8	42	468
9	43	468
10	44	468
11	45	468
12	46	468
13	47	468
14	48	468
15	49	468
26	60	468
27	61	468
28	62	468
29	63	468
30	64	468
31	65	26,325

Notice major jump between years 30 and 31:

CUMULATIVE ANNUAL PREMIUM #	DEATH BENEFIT ##
468	250,000
935	250,000
1,403	250,000
1,870	250,000
2,338	250,000
2,805	250,000
3,273	250,000
3,740	250,000
4,208	250,000
4,675	250,000
5,143	250,000
5,610	250,000
6,078	250,000
6,545	250,000
7,013	250,000
12,155	250,000
12,623	250,000
13,090	250,000
13,558	250,000
14,025	250,000
40,350	250,000

APPENDIX C1
FULL PAY WITH PARTIAL PUA - MALE, AGE 50
Whole Life 95 Illustration

		Guaranteed		
POL YR	AGE AT START OF YEAR	BASE POLICY ANNUAL PREM #	BASE GUAR. CASH VALUE ##	END OF YEAR DIVIDEND ## *
1	50	2,853	106	0
2	51	2,853	2,493	402
3	52	2,853	4,565	453
4	53	2,853	6,684	457
5	54	2,853	8,846	517
6	55	2,853	11,044	581
7	56	2,853	13,279	649
8	57	2,853	15,554	719
9	58	2,853	17,883	783
10	59	2,853	20,265	851
11	60	2,853	22,320	926
12	61	2,853	24,392	1,011
13	62	2,853	26,469	1,106
14	63	2,853	28,547	1,278
15	64	2,853	30,625	1,452
66	115	0	100,000	34,889
67	116	0	100,000	36,651
68	117	0	100,000	38,502
69	118	0	100,000	40,446
70	119	0	100,000	42,489
71	120	0	100,000	44,634

Busting the Life Insurance Lies

Concept Based on the 2016 Dividend Scale

Non-Guaranteed

NET AFTER TAX OUTLAY # *	CUM NET A/T OUTLAY # *	CASH VALUE OF ALL ADDS ## *	NET CASH VALUE ## *	NET DEATH BENEFIT ## *
3,264	3,264	403	509	101,116
3,264	6,528	1,222	3,715	102,598
3,264	9,791	2,117	6,682	104,773
3,264	13,055	3,044	9,728	106,966
3,264	16,319	4,060	12,906	109,157
3,264	19,583	5,169	16,213	111,434
3,264	22,846	6,378	19,657	113,798
3,264	26,110	7,691	23,245	116,254
3,264	29,374	9,104	26,987	118,791
3,264	32,638	10,625	30,890	121,398
3,264	35,901	12,260	34,580	124,081
3,264	39,165	14,021	38,413	126,854
3,264	42,429	15,917	42,386	129,732
3,264	45,693	18,025	46,572	132,795
3,264	48,957	20,354	50,979	136,108
0	139,149	626,752	726,752	726,752
0	139,149	663,403	763,403	763,403
0	139,149	701,904	801,904	801,904
0	139,149	742,351	842,351	842,351
0	139,149	784,839	884,839	884,839
0	139,149	829,474	929,474	929,474

APPENDIX C2

MAX PUA'S WITH NATURAL VANISH - MALE, AGE 50

Whole Life 95 Illustration

Guaranteed

POL YR	AGE AT START OF YEAR	BASE POLICY ANNUAL PREM #	BASE GUAR. CASH VALUE ##	END OF YEAR DIVIDEND ## *
1	50	2,853	106	0
2	51	2,853	2,493	468
3	52	2,853	4,565	556
4	53	2,853	6,684	600
5	54	2,853	8,846	705
6	55	2,853	11,044	817
7	56	2,853	13,279	938
8	57	2,853	15,554	980
9	58	2,853	17,883	1,011
10	59	2,853	20,265	1,043
11	60	2,853	22,320	1,080
12	61	2,853	24,392	1,124
13	62	2,853	26,469	1,175
14	63	2,853	28,547	1,299
15	64	2,853	30,625	1,420
66	115	0	100,000	13,396
67	116	0	100,000	14,072
68	117	0	100,000	14,783
69	118	0	100,000	15,530
70	119	0	100,000	16,314
71	120	0	100,000	17,138

Busting the Life Insurance Lies

Concept Based on the 2016 Dividend Scale

Non-Guaranteed

NET AFTER TAX OUTLAY # *	CUM NET A/T OUTLAY # *	CASH VALUE OF ALL ADDS ## *	NET CASH VALUE ## *	NET DEATH BENEFIT ## *
5,906	5,906	2,996	3,102	108,292
5,906	11,812	6,557	9,050	116,788
5,906	17,718	10,320	14,885	125,905
5,906	23,624	14,245	20,929	134,923
5,906	29,530	18,392	27,238	143,834
5,906	35,436	22,769	33,813	152,739
5,906	41,342	27,391	40,670	161,653
0	41,342	26,249	41,803	157,289
0	41,342	25,097	42,980	153,135
0	41,342	23,936	44,201	149,170
0	41,342	22,769	45,089	145,391
0	41,342	21,602	45,994	141,802
0	41,342	20,440	46,909	138,409
0	41,342	19,356	47,903	135,281
0	41,342	18,354	48,979	132,467
0	41,342	179,652	279,652	279,652
0	41,342	193,724	293,724	293,724
0	41,342	208,508	308,508	308,508
0	41,342	224,037	324,037	324,037
0	41,342	240,351	340,351	340,351
0	41,342	257,489	357,489	357,489

* Natural vanish / offset

APPENDIX C3

NO PUA - MALE, AGE 50
Whole Life 95 Illustration

		Guaranteed		
POL YR	AGE AT START OF YEAR	BASE POLICY ANNUAL PREM #	BASE GUAR. CASH VALUE ##	END OF YEAR DIVIDEND ## *
1	50	2,853	106	0
2	51	2,853	2,493	392
3	52	2,853	4,565	437
4	53	2,853	6,684	434
5	54	2,853	8,846	488
6	55	2,853	11,044	544
7	56	2,853	13,279	604
8	57	2,853	15,554	666
9	58	2,853	17,883	721
10	59	2,853	20,265	779
11	60	2,853	22,320	843
12	61	2,853	24,392	917
13	62	2,853	26,469	999
14	63	2,853	28,547	1,157
15	64	2,853	30,625	1,317
66	115	0	100,000	30,318
67	116	0	100,000	31,849
68	117	0	100,000	33,458
69	118	0	100,000	35,147
70	119	0	100,000	36,922
71	120	0	100,000	38,787

Concept Based on the 2016 Dividend Scale

Non-Guaranteed

NET AFTER TAX OUTLAY # *	CUM NET A/T OUTLAY # *	CASH VALUE OF ALL ADDS ## *	NET CASH VALUE ## *	NET DEATH BENEFIT ## *
2,853	2,853	0	106	100,000
2,853	5,706	392	2,885	100,392
2,853	8,559	842	5,407	101,488
2,853	11,412	1,303	7,987	102,620
2,853	14,265	1,832	10,678	103,766
2,853	17,118	2,433	13,477	105,012
2,853	19,971	3,111	16,390	106,358
2,853	22,824	3,870	19,424	107,806
2,853	25,677	4,705	22,588	109,344
2,853	28,530	5,623	25,888	110,962
2,853	31,383	6,629	28,949	112,663
2,853	34,236	7,734	32,126	114,459
2,853	37,089	8,948	35,417	116,362
2,853	39,942	10,346	38,893	118,451
2,853	42,795	11,936	42,561	120,788
0	128,385	531,666	631,666	631,666
0	128,385	563,515	663,515	663,515
0	128,385	596,972	696,972	696,972
0	128,385	632,119	732,119	732,119
0	128,385	669,042	769,042	769,042
0	128,385	707,828	807,828	807,828

APPENDIX C4

MODIFIED ENDOWMENT CONTRACT (MEC)
YEAR ONE - MALE, AGE 50
Whole Life 95 Illustration

		Guaranteed		
POL YR	AGE AT START OF YEAR	BASE POLICY ANNUAL PREM #	BASE GUAR. CASH VALUE ##	END OF YEAR DIVIDEND ## *
1	50	27,630	1,060	0
2	51	27,630	24,930	5,425
3	52	27,630	45,650	6,483
4	53	27,630	66,840	7,557
5	54	27,630	88,460	8,824
6	55	27,630	110,440	10,171
7	56	27,630	132,790	11,623
8	57	27,630	155,540	13,160
9	58	27,630	178,830	14,650
10	59	27,630	202,650	16,237
11	60	27,630	223,200	17,961
12	61	27,630	243,920	19,924
13	62	27,630	264,690	22,091
14	63	27,630	285,470	25,118
15	64	27,630	306,250	28,271
66	115	0	1,000,000	751,328
67	116	0	1,000,000	789,270
68	117	0	1,000,000	829,128
69	118	0	1,000,000	870,999
70	119	0	1,000,000	914,985
71	120	0	1,000,000	961,191

Busting the Life Insurance Lies

Concept Based on the 2016 Dividend Scale

Non-Guaranteed

NET AFTER TAX OUTLAY # *	CUM NET A/T OUTLAY # *	CASH VALUE OF ALL ADDS ## *	NET CASH VALUE ## *	NET DEATH BENEFIT ## *
70,000	70,000	41,577	42,637	1,115,083
70,000	140,000	89,932	114,862	1,231,922
70,000	210,000	140,885	186,535	1,355,406
70,000	280,000	194,496	261,336	1,477,808
70,000	350,000	250,982	339,442	1,599,339
70,000	420,000	310,431	420,871	1,720,358
70,000	490,000	373,005	505,795	1,841,071
70,000	560,000	438,805	594,345	1,961,672
70,000	630,000	507,948	686,778	2,082,186
70,000	700,000	580,558	783,208	2,202,584
70,000	770,000	656,782	879,982	2,323,061
70,000	840,000	736,793	980,713	2,443,951
70,000	910,000	820,715	1,085,405	2,565,654
70,000	980,000	909,365	1,194,835	2,689,175
70,000	1,050,000	1,002,960	1,309,210	2,815,346
0	2,100,000	14,630,100	15,630,100	15,630,100
0	2,100,000	15,419,370	16,419,370	16,419,370
0	2,100,000	16,248,498	17,248,498	17,248,498
0	2,100,000	17,119,498	18,119,498	18,119,498
0	2,100,000	18,034,482	19,034,482	19,034,482
0	2,100,000	18,995,673	19,995,673	19,995,673

APPENDIX D1

FULL PAY WITH PARTIAL PUA - MALE, AGE 75
Whole Life 121 Illustration

		Guaranteed		
POL YR	AGE AT START OF YEAR	BASE POLICY ANNUAL PREM #	BASE GUAR. CASH VALUE ##	END OF YEAR DIVIDEND ## *
1	75	6,826	0	0
2	76	6,826	3,756	123
3	77	6,826	8,559	308
4	78	6,826	13,267	461
5	79	6,826	17,843	680
6	80	6,826	22,285	901
7	81	6,826	26,558	1,137
8	82	6,826	30,690	1,362
9	83	6,826	34,686	1,582
10	84	6,826	38,533	1,788
11	85	6,826	42,200	1,996
12	86	6,826	45,664	2,135
13	87	6,826	48,906	2,298
14	88	6,826	51,918	2,423
15	89	6,826	54,697	2,532
41	115	6,826	90,527	998
42	116	6,826	91,294	980
43	117	6,826	92,031	964
44	118	6,826	92,747	952
45	119	6,826	93,375	945
46	120	6,826	100,000	891

Busting the Life Insurance Lies

Concept Based on the 2016 Dividend Scale
Endowment: Cash Value Death Benefit

Non-Guaranteed

NET AFTER TAX OUTLAY # *	CUM NET A/T OUTLAY # *	CASH VALUE OF ALL ADDS ## *	NET CASH VALUE ## *	NET DEATH BENEFIT ## *
7,374	7,374	531	531	100,755
7,374	14,748	1,196	4,952	101,618
7,374	22,123	2,058	10,617	102,699
7,374	29,497	3,089	16,356	103,984
7,374	36,871	4,354	22,197	105,518
7,374	44,245	5,859	28,144	107,321
7,374	51,620	7,620	34,178	109,398
7,374	58,994	9,629	40,319	111,735
7,374	66,368	11,880	46,566	114,317
7,374	73,742	14,362	52,895	117,123
7,374	81,116	17,073	59,273	120,147
7,374	88,491	19,945	65,609	123,316
7,374	95,865	22,994	71,900	126,637
7,374	103,239	26,182	78,100	130,077
7,374	110,613	29,487	84,184	133,612
6,826	286,731	84,358	174,885	186,737
6,826	293,557	85,533	176,827	187,746
6,826	300,383	86,686	178,717	188,736
6,826	307,209	87,831	180,578	189,711
6,826	314,035	88,939	182,314	190,677
6,826	320,861	91,586	191,586	191,586

APPENDIX D2

MAX PUA'S WITH NATURAL VANISH - MALE, AGE 75

Whole Life 121 Illustration

		Guaranteed		
POL YR	AGE AT START OF YEAR	BASE POLICY ANNUAL PREM #	BASE GUAR. CASH VALUE ##	END OF YEAR DIVIDEND ## *
1	75	6,826	0	0
2	76	6,826	3,756	374
3	77	6,826	8,559	699
4	78	6,826	13,267	1,004
5	79	6,826	17,843	1,385
6	80	6,826	22,285	1,781
7	81	6,826	26,558	2,204
8	82	6,826	30,690	2,625
9	83	6,826	34,686	3,050
10	84	6,826	38,533	3,469
11	85	6,826	42,200	3,809
12	86	6,826	45,664	4,066
13	87	6,826	48,906	4,356
14	88	6,826	51,918	4,600
15	89	6,826	54,697	4,913
41	115	6,826	90,527	494
42	116	6,826	91,294	408
43	117	6,826	92,031	326
44	118	6,826	92,747	249
45	119	6,826	93,375	176
46	120	6,826	100,000	100

Busting the Life Insurance Lies

Concept Based on the 2016 Dividend Scale
Endowment: Cash Value Equals Death Benefit

Non-Guaranteed

NET AFTER TAX OUTLAY # *	* CUM NET A/T OUTLAY # *	CASH VALUE OF ALL ADDS ## *	NET CASH VALUE ## *	NET DEATH BENEFIT ## *
13,939	13,939	6,898	6,898	109,801
13,939	27,878	14,306	18,062	119,776
13,939	41,817	22,175	30,734	130,033
13,939	55,756	30,481	43,748	140,522
13,939	69,695	39,293	57,136	151,308
13,939	83,634	48,620	70,905	162,427
13,939	97,573	58,479	85,037	173,905
13,939	111,512	68,867	99,557	185,744
13,939	125,451	79,786	114,472	197,941
13,933	139,384	91,212	129,745	210,480
9,860	149,244	99,135	141,335	218,566
9,860	159,104	107,331	152,995	226,879
9,860	168,964	115,813	164,719	235,433
9,860	178,824	124,529	176,447	244,190
13,939	192,763	137,443	192,140	257,722
0	192,763	40,926	131,453	142,080
0	192,763	34,583	125,877	135,477
0	192,763	28,139	120,170	128,804
0	192,763	21,604	114,351	122,066
0	192,763	14,976	108,351	115,268
0	192,763	8,406	108,406	108,406

* Endowment

APPENDIX D3

NO PUA - MALE, AGE 75

Whole Life 121 Illustration

			Guaranteed	
POL YR	AGE AT START OF YEAR	BASE POLICY ANNUAL PREM #	BASE GUAR. CASH VALUE ##	END OF YEAR DIVIDEND ## *
1	75	6,826	0	0
2	76	6,826	3,756	102
3	77	6,826	8,559	275
4	78	6,826	13,267	416
5	79	6,826	17,843	621
6	80	6,826	22,285	828
7	81	6,826	26,558	1,048
8	82	6,826	30,690	1,257
9	83	6,826	34,686	1,459
10	84	6,826	38,533	1,648
11	85	6,826	42,200	1,837
12	86	6,826	45,664	1,959
13	87	6,826	48,906	2,103
14	88	6,826	51,918	2,210
15	89	6,826	54,697	2,301
41	115	6,826	90,527	782
42	116	6,826	91,294	768
43	117	6,826	92,031	756
44	118	6,826	92,747	746
45	119	6,826	93,375	741
46	120	6,826	100,000	698

Busting the Life Insurance Lies

Concept Based on the 2016 Dividend Scale
Endowment: Cash Value Equals Death Benefit

Non-Guaranteed

NET AFTER TAX OUTLAY # *	* CUM NET A/T OUTLAY # *	CASH VALUE OF ALL ADDS ## *	NET CASH VALUE ## *	NET DEATH BENEFIT ## *
6,826	6,826	0	0	100,000
6,826	13,652	102	3,858	100,102
6,826	20,478	379	8,938	100,417
6,826	27,304	802	14,069	100,934
6,826	34,130	1,437	19,280	101,696
6,826	40,956	2,290	24,575	102,720
6,826	47,782	3,375	29,933	104,012
6,826	54,608	4,683	35,373	105,556
6,826	61,434	6,211	40,897	107,335
6,826	68,260	7,945	46,478	109,328
6,826	75,086	9,886	52,086	111,527
6,826	81,912	11,966	57,630	113,861
6,826	88,738	14,205	63,111	116,335
6,826	95,564	16,562	68,480	118,915
6,826	102,390	19,020	73,717	121,578

6,826	279,866	65,695	156,222	167,548
6,826	286,692	66,615	157,909	168,338
6,826	293,518	67,517	159,548	169,114
6,826	300,344	68,413	161,160	169,878
6,826	307,170	69,280	162,655	170,634
6,826	313,996	71,347	171,347	171,347

* Endowment

APPENDIX E1-1

INFORCE FULL PAY - MALE, AGE 47
Whole Life 100 Inforce Illustration

			Guaranteed	
POL YR	CAL YEAR BEG	AGE AT START OF YEAR	BASE POLICY ANNUAL PREM #	BASE GUAR. CASH VALUE ##
16	2016	62	7,186	102,764
17	2017	63	7,186	110,764
18	2018	64	7,186	118,776
19	2019	65	7,186	126,799
20	2020	66	7,186	134,838
21	2021	67	7,186	142,286
22	2022	68	7,186	149,724
23	2023	69	7,186	157,149
24	2024	70	7,186	164,530
25	2025	71	7,186	171,844
26	2026	72	7,186	179,038
27	2027	73	7,186	186,062
28	2028	74	7,186	192,885
29	2029	75	7,186	199,491
30	2030	76	7,186	205,893
31	2031	77	7,186	212,111
32	2032	78	7,186	218,193
33	2033	79	7,186	224,150
34	2034	80	7,186	229,988
35	2035	81	7,186	235,672
36	2036	82	7,186	241,165
37	2037	83	7,186	246,407
38	2038	84	7,186	251,373
39	2039	85	7,186	256,071
40	2040	86	7,186	260,532

Concept Based on the 2016 Dividend Scale

Non-Guaranteed

END OF YEAR DIVIDEND ## *	NET AFTER TAX OUTLAY # *	CASH VALUE OF ALL ADDS ## *	NET CASH VALUE ## *	NET DEATH BENEFIT ## *
3,374	0 *	39,195	141,960	399,793
3,762	7,500	43,907	154,671	406,048
4,194	7,500	49,139	167,915	412,866
4,654	7,186	54,924	181,723	420,282
5,143	7,186	61,299	196,137	428,315
5,650	7,186	68,290	210,576	436,976
6,166	7,186	75,916	225,641	446,258
6,714	7,186	84,216	241,365	456,173
7,277	7,186	93,208	257,738	466,727
7,879	7,186	102,928	274,773	477,941
8,382	7,186	113,272	292,310	489,710
8,971	7,186	124,311	310,373	502,061
9,626	7,186	136,104	328,989	515,080
10,302	7,186	148,662	348,153	528,794
10,970	7,186	161,981	367,874	543,188
11,586	7,186	176,015	388,126	558,192
12,118	7,186	190,695	408,888	573,695
12,596	7,186	205,973	430,123	589,607
13,084	7,186	221,854	451,842	605,915
13,584	7,186	238,335	474,007	622,628
14,185	7,186	255,485	496,650	639,845
14,876	7,186	273,359	519,766	657,673
15,588	7,186	291,953	543,326	676,149
16,263	7,186	311,216	567,287	695,235
16,725	7,186	330,947	591,478	714,711

*Year 16 premium already paid

APPENDIX E1-2
INFORCE FULL PAY - MALE, AGE 47 (CONTINUED)
Whole Life 100 Inforce Illustration

			Guaranteed	
POL YR	CAL YEAR BEG	AGE AT START OF YEAR	BASE POLICY ANNUAL PREM #	BASE GUAR. CASH VALUE ##
41	2041	87	7,186	264,798
42	2042	88	7,186	268,942
43	2043	89	7,186	273,032
44	2044	90	7,186	277,165
45	2045	91	7,186	281,449
46	2046	92	7,186	286,010
47	2047	93	7,186	291,028
48	2048	94	7,186	296,619
49	2049	95	7,186	302,840
50	2050	96	7,186	309,620
51	2051	97	7,186	316,750
52	2052	98	7,186	323,690
53	2053	99	7,186	334,139

Busting the Life Insurance Lies

Non-Guaranteed

END OF YEAR DIVIDEND ## *	NET AFTER TAX OUTLAY # *	CASH VALUE OF ALL ADDS ## *	NET CASH VALUE ## *	NET DEATH BENEFIT ## *
17,007	7,186	350,985	615,784	734,360
17,147	7,186	371,225	640,167	754,013
17,275	7,186	391,700	664,732	773,644
17,215	7,186	412,298	689,463	793,064
17,030	7,186	432,984	714,432	812,126
16,754	7,186	453,793	739,802	830,723
16,394	7,186	474,825	765,853	848,757
16,359	7,186	496,530	793,148	866,539
16,517	7,186	519,194	822,034	884,277
17,070	7,186	543,181	852,801	902,364
17,760	7,186	568,475	885,225	920,937
17,972	7,186	593,989	917,679	939,500
8,973	7,186	614,688	948,827	948,827

APPENDIX E2

HALF DEATH BENEFIT SAMPLE - MALE, AGE 47
Whole Life 100 Inforce Illustration

POL YR	CAL YEAR BEG	AGE AT START OF YEAR	BASE POLICY ANNUAL PREM #	BASE GUAR. CASH VALUE ##
			Guaranteed	
16	2016	62	7,186	102,764
17	2017	63	3,609	55,382
18	2018	64	3,609	59,388
19	2019	65	3,609	63,400
20	2020	66	3,609	67,419
21	2021	67	3,609	71,143
22	2022	68	3,609	74,862
23	2023	69	3,609	78,575
24	2024	70	3,609	82,265
25	2025	71	3,609	85,922
26	2026	72	3,609	89,519
27	2027	73	3,609	93,031
28	2028	74	3,609	96,443
29	2029	75	3,609	99,746
46	2046	92	3,609	143,005
47	2047	93	3,609	145,515
48	2048	94	3,609	148,310
49	2049	95	3,609	151,421
50	2050	96	3,609	154,810
51	2051	97	3,609	158,376
52	2052	98	3,609	161,846
53	2053	99	3,609	167,070

Busting the Life Insurance Lies

Concept Based on the 2016 Dividend Scale

Non-Guaranteed

END OF YEAR DIVIDEND ## *	NET AFTER TAX OUTLAY # *	CASH VALUE OF ALL ADDS ## *	NET CASH VALUE ## *	NET DEATH BENEFIT ## *
3,374	0	39,195	141,960	399,793
3,186	3,766	95,959	151,341	327,739
3,482	3,766	101,707	161,095	333,443
3,796	3,609	107,844	171,244	339,531
4,131	3,609	114,394	181,814	346,020
4,480	3,609	121,377	192,520	352,918
4,835	3,609	128,807	203,669	360,223
5,213	3,609	136,710	215,285	367,946
5,603	3,609	145,096	227,361	376,093
6,019	3,609	153,982	239,904	384,679
6,387	3,609	163,304	252,823	393,654
6,817	3,609	173,102	266,133	403,046
7,292	3,609	183,412	279,855	412,916
7,785	3,609	194,238	293,984	423,286
12,594	3,609	440,838	583,844	649,839
12,339	3,609	457,683	603,198	663,410
12,322	3,609	475,159	623,468	676,804
12,445	3,609	493,486	644,906	690,169
12,855	3,609	512,915	667,726	703,790
13,365	3,609	533,395	691,771	717,767
13,528	3,609	554,000	715,845	731,740
6,977	3,609	571,914	738,984	738,984

APPENDIX E3

NUMBERS PROVING REDUCED PAID UP (RPU) MALE, AGE 47

Whole Life 100 Inforce Illustration

			Guaranteed	
POL YR	CAL YEAR BEG	AGE AT START OF YEAR	BASE POLICY ANNUAL PREM #	BASE GUAR. CASH VALUE ##
16	2016	62	7,186	102,764
17	2017	63	0	105,255
18	2018	64	0	107,740
19	2019	65	0	110,220
20	2020	66	0	112,693
21	2021	67	0	115,159
22	2022	68	0	117,621
23	2023	69	0	120,078
24	2024	70	0	122,522
25	2025	71	0	124,943
26	2026	72	0	127,325
27	2027	73	0	129,649
28	2028	74	0	131,909
29	2029	75	0	134,096
30	2030	76	0	136,215
46	2046	92	0	162,737
47	2047	93	0	164,401
48	2048	94	0	166,252
49	2049	95	0	168,310
50	2050	96	0	170,552
51	2051	97	0	172,918
52	2052	98	0	175,212
53	2053	99	0	178,671

Busting the Life Insurance Lies

Concept Based on the 2016 Dividend Scale

		Non-Guaranteed		
END OF YEAR DIVIDEND ## *	NET AFTER TAX OUTLAY # *	CASH VALUE OF ALL ADDS ## *	NET CASH VALUE ## *	NET DEATH BENEFIT ## *
3,374	0	39,195	141,960	399,793
2,611	0	42,756	148,011	249,429
2,769	0	46,535	154,275	254,019
2,938	0	50,544	160,764	258,780
3,119	0	54,797	167,490	263,724
3,309	0	59,305	174,464	268,859
3,504	0	64,077	181,698	274,188
3,712	0	69,127	189,205	279,719
3,928	0	74,462	196,984	285,458
4,158	0	80,092	205,035	291,416
4,392	0	86,011	213,336	297,597
4,662	0	92,243	221,892	304,030
4,959	0	98,810	230,720	310,752
5,269	0	105,717	239,814	317,778
5,577	0	112,965	249,180	325,107
8,433	0	265,147	427,884	468,953
8,284	0	276,141	440,542	478,063
8,286	0	287,536	453,787	487,067
8,372	0	299,468	467,778	496,059
8,640	0	312,098	482,650	505,214
8,970	0	325,397	498,315	514,596
9,084	0	338,798	514,010	523,978
4,982	0	350,469	529,140	529,140

APPENDIX F1

SAMPLE OF A UL "DYING ON THE VINE" OR IMPLODING ILLUSTRATION

Policy Value	EOY Age	Planned Premium
31	78	2,048
32	79	2,048
33	80	2,048
34	81	2,048
35	82	2,048
36	83	2,048
37	84	2,048
38	85	2,048
39	86	2,048
40	87	2,048
41	88	2,048
42	89	2,048
43	90	2,048
44	91	2,048
45	92	2,048
46	93	2,048
47	94	2,048
48	95	2,048
49	96	2,048
50	97	2,048
51	98	2,048
52	99	2,048
53	100	2,048
54	101	171
55	102	0
56	103	0

Male, Original Age 47

End of Year Non-Guaranteed Assumptions
5.05% Initial Assumed Rate, Current Charges

Policy Value	Net Surrender Value	Net Death Benefit
32,235	32,235	250,000
34,024	34,024	250,000
35,835	35,835	250,000
37,665	37,665	250,000
39,504	39,504	250,000
41,345	41,345	250,000
43,172	43,172	250,000
44,965	44,965	250,000
46,701	46,701	250,000
48,359	48,359	250,000
49,921	49,921	250,000
51,362	51,362	250,000
52,642	52,642	250,000
53,756	53,756	250,000
54,691	54,691	250,000
55,425	55,425	250,000
55,913	55,913	250,000
56,082	56,082	250,000
55,829	55,829	250,000
55,047	55,047	250,000
53,544	53,544	250,000
51,011	51,011	250,000
46,973	46,973	250,000
39,825	39,825	250,000
21,164	21,164	250,000
##	##	##

APPENDIX F2

SAMPLE OF A UL "DYING ON THE VINE" OR IMPLODING ILLUSTRATION

			Guaranteed Values	
Policy Year	Age	End of Year Account Values	End of Year Cash Surrender Values	Beginning of Year Death Benefit
22	50	14,293.70	719	100,719
23	51	14,896.70	1,322	100,719
24	52	15,478.87	1,904	101,322
25	53	16,032.00	2,457	101,904
26	54	16,548.92	2,974	102,457
27	55	17,018.96	3,444	102,974
28	56	17,432.77	3,858	103,444
29	57	17,780.03	4,205	103,858
30	58	18,052.77	4,478	104,205
31	59	18,240.81	4,666	104,478
32	60	18,328.13	4,754	104,666
33	61	18,298.34	4,724	104,754
34	62	18,133.10	4,559	104,724
35	63	17,808.40	4,234	104,559
36	64	17,295.58	3,721	104,234
37	65	16,563.90	2,989	103,721
38	66	15,600.47	2,026	102,989
39	67	14,361.75	787	102,026
40	68	Lapsed	Lapsed	Lapsed
41	69			
52	80			
53	81			
54	82			
55	83			

Male, Original Age 28

**Total Values Including
Non-Guaranteed Assumptions ****

End of Year Account Values	End of Year Cash Surrender Values	Beginning of Year Death Benefit
14,670.11	1,096	101,096
15,675.15	2,101	101,096
16,677.49	3,103	102,101
17,694.30	4,120	103,103
18,735.22	5,161	104,120
19,800.63	6,226	105,161
20,877.53	7,303	106,226
21,945.42	8,371	107,303
22,998.54	9,424	108,371
24,027.64	10,453	109,424
25,021.22	11,447	110,453
25,968.36	12,394	111,447
26,859.37	13,285	112,394
27,683.05	14,108	113,285
28,477.17	14,903	114,108
29,244.20	15,670	114,903
29,995.11	16,421	115,670
30,664.86	17,090	116,421
31,243.33	17,669	117,090
31,721.38	18,147	117,669
21,658.68	8,084	110,944
18,213.20	4,639	108,084
14,100.01	525	104,639
Lapsed	Lapsed	Lapsed

Appendix G
THE WHOLE TRUTH ABOUT WHOLE LIFE
Male, Age 35

Kim: Hello. I'm Kim Butler. Whole life insurance can be a very emotional product. For some reason, even though it's been around for centuries it has a lot of negative connotations to it. But the bottom line is really, what is the net, net, net, internal rate of return earning on your cash value?

That's a hard thing to figure out. In this video you'll learn the internal rate of return after the cost of commission, after the cost of the death benefit and after the cost of running the company. Stay tuned for what will probably be a surprise.

Todd: Let's look at a Funding calculator from www.truthconcepts.com. I want to see the actual effects of what's going on and this calculator is what we'll use to do that. So let's look at a 35-year old, let's go out to age 70, open up the stored life insurance data and let's use our 35-year old right there.

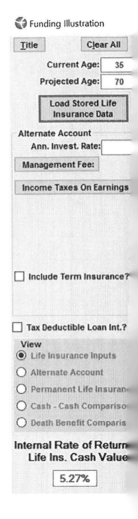

Go ahead and pull some level term in there too. Alright so when we look at this, we see an internal rate of return on this policy of 5.27%. That's not real exciting for a lot of people and I think that's part of the problem with life insurance is it's not sexy enough.

www.truthconcepts.com

Clear PLI   NEW

Permanent Life Insurance						
Age	Premium	Ann. Loan	Loan Int.	Loan Pmt	Net CV	Net DB
35	(26,720)				14,691	1,067,330
36	(26,720)				30,244	1,133,876
37	(26,720)				57,666	1,208,114
38	(26,720)				88,520	1,281,955
39	(26,720)				120,981	1,355,469
40	(26,720)				155,156	1,428,897
41	(26,720)				191,091	1,502,219
42	(26,720)				228,876	1,575,624
43	(26,720)				268,639	1,649,360
44	(26,720)				310,464	1,723,659
45	(26,720)				354,443	1,798,578
46	(26,720)				400,675	1,874,053
47	(26,720)				449,317	1,950,316
48	(26,720)				500,513	2,026,885
49	(26,720)				554,380	2,103,900
50	(26,720)				610,995	2,184,635
51	(26,720)				671,687	2,269,224
52	(26,720)				736,721	2,358,084
53	(26,720)				806,337	2,451,354
54	(26,720)				880,780	2,549,332
55	(26,720)				959,673	2,650,873
56	(26,720)				1,043,265	2,756,007
57	(26,720)				1,131,767	2,864,886
58	(26,720)				1,225,432	2,976,827
59	(26,720)				1,324,436	3,091,943
60	(26,720)				1,428,936	3,210,398
61	(26,720)				1,539,406	3,333,279
62	(26,720)				1,656,183	3,461,380
63	(26,720)				1,779,543	3,595,023
64	(26,720)				1,909,794	3,734,189
65					2,020,206	3,830,690

Kim: Will you explain what you are showing here?

Todd: Here we've got a $26,720 payment premium plus PUA payment for 30 years and then we stop making those payments and then as we scroll down we see that the cash value grows to $2,666,000 and the death benefit grows to $4,385,000 over that timeframe.

Todd: Okay, so 5.27, we need to understand what that 5.27 is. That is a safe, liquid return. What fits in that same asset class?

Participant: Cash.

Todd: In your mattress, right? Let me see, is it doing—no, no, not quite 5.27. At the bank they are charging for the money sitting in there. I guess you could argue CDs are semi-liquid depending on the timeframe of your CD. Money markets, savings accounts, you know all of that if you believe in the FDIC, treasuries if you believe in the federal government. Are they doing anywhere near 5.27?

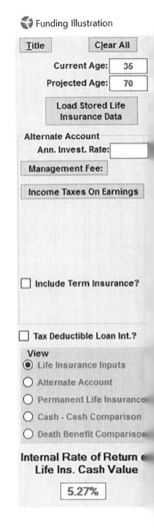

Busting the Life Insurance Lies

	Clear PLI					NEW

Permanent Life Insurance

Age	Premium	Ann. Loan	Loan Int.	Loan Pmt	Net CV	Net DB
41	(26,720)				191,091	1,502,219
42	(26,720)				228,876	1,575,624
43	(26,720)				268,639	1,649,360
44	(26,720)				310,464	1,723,659
45	(26,720)				354,443	1,798,578
46	(26,720)				400,675	1,874,053
47	(26,720)				449,317	1,950,316
48	(26,720)				500,513	2,026,885
49	(26,720)				554,380	2,103,900
50	(26,720)				610,995	2,184,635
51	(26,720)				671,687	2,269,224
52	(26,720)				736,721	2,358,084
53	(26,720)				806,337	2,451,354
54	(26,720)				880,780	2,549,332
55	(26,720)				959,673	2,650,873
56	(26,720)				1,043,265	2,756,007
57	(26,720)				1,131,767	2,864,886
58	(26,720)				1,225,432	2,976,827
59	(26,720)				1,324,436	3,091,943
60	(26,720)				1,428,936	3,210,398
61	(26,720)				1,539,406	3,333,279
62	(26,720)				1,656,183	3,461,380
63	(26,720)				1,779,543	3,595,023
64	(26,720)				1,909,794	3,734,189
65					2,020,206	3,830,690
66					2,136,581	3,932,324
67					2,259,231	4,038,735
68					2,388,347	4,149,963
69					2,524,200	4,265,652
70					2,666,675	4,385,699

Safe, liquid asset, this needs to be looked at as more of a savings vehicle than investment vehicle. That is great, great for something in that asset class. But the items that we compare against: savings accounts, checking accounts, money markets, CDs, all these things, do we have to pay taxes on those annually? If we look at that, income tax let's use our 35%, that's fine. At 35% what this is saying is we would have to earn 8.11.

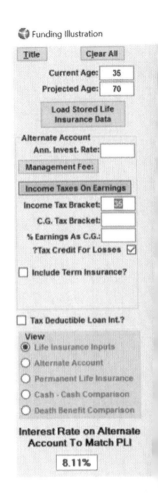

Clear PLI **NEW**

Age	Premium	Ann. Loan	Loan Int.	Loan Pmt	Net CV	Net DB
41	(26,720)				191,091	1,502,219
42	(26,720)				228,876	1,575,624
43	(26,720)				268,639	1,649,360
44	(26,720)				310,464	1,723,659
45	(26,720)				354,443	1,798,578
46	(26,720)				400,675	1,874,053
47	(26,720)				449,317	1,950,316
48	(26,720)				500,513	2,026,885
49	(26,720)				554,380	2,103,900
50	(26,720)				610,995	2,184,635
51	(26,720)				671,687	2,269,224
52	(26,720)				736,721	2,358,084
53	(26,720)				806,337	2,451,354
54	(26,720)				880,780	2,549,332
55	(26,720)				959,673	2,650,873
56	(26,720)				1,043,265	2,756,007
57	(26,720)				1,131,767	2,864,886
58	(26,720)				1,225,432	2,976,827
59	(26,720)				1,324,436	3,091,943
60	(26,720)				1,428,936	3,210,398
61	(26,720)				1,539,406	3,333,279
62	(26,720)				1,656,183	3,461,380
63	(26,720)				1,779,543	3,595,023
64	(26,720)				1,909,794	3,734,189
65					2,020,206	3,830,690
66					2,136,581	3,932,324
67					2,259,231	4,038,735
68					2,388,347	4,149,963
69					2,524,200	4,265,652
70					2,666,675	4,385,699

Wait a second, back up, take that income tax off for just a minute. Let's copy this 5.27 and let's make sure we understand how this works. So what I'm saying is, if we chose not to put money in the life insurance policy but instead put it another asset, let's say we found one that could do 5.27% every year.

Now I know Mr. Client you've looked at your illustration and you know it's not earning 5.27 every year because the

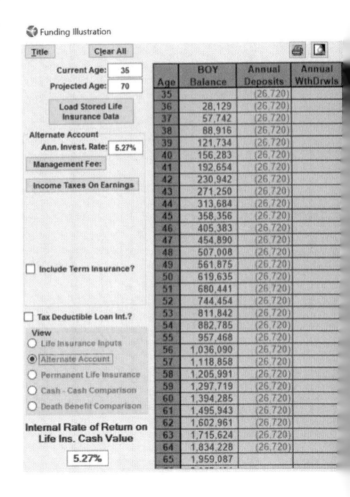

first years it's negative until it turns and straightens up and starts earning, right? But the internal return over 35 years is 5.27 if we take this and we look at an alternate account, so click on alternate account for just a minute, and we look at the same cash flow going somewhere else earning 5.27 not the last year but every single year.

Annual RePmts	Annual Int. Rate	Annual Interest	EOY Balance
	5.27 %	1,409	28,129
	5.27 %	2,893	57,742
	5.27 %	4,454	88,916
	5.27 %	6,098	121,734
	5.27 %	7,829	156,283
	5.27 %	9,651	192,654
	5.27 %	11,569	
	5.27 %	13,588	
	5.27 %	15,714	
	5.27 %	17,951	
	5.27 %	20,307	
	5.27 %	22,787	
	5.27 %	25,398	
	5.27 %	28,147	
	5.27 %	31,040	
	5.27 %	34,086	
	5.27 %	37,293	
	5.27 %	40,668	
	5.27 %	44,222	
	5.27 %	47,963	
	5.27 %	51,902	
	5.27 %	56,048	
	5.27 %	60,413	1,205,991
	5.27 %	65,008	1,297,719
	5.27 %	69,845	1,394,285
	5.27 %	74,938	1,495,943
	5.27 %	80,299	1,602,961
	5.27 %	85,943	1,715,624
	5.27 %	91,884	1,834,228
	5.27 %	98,139	1,959,087
	5.27 %	103,314	2,062,401

NEW

Notes   TOP

Zoom% 100   B / A Text

Cash Value at age 70

$2,666,675

If we scroll down we see the same $2,666,000, does that make sense?

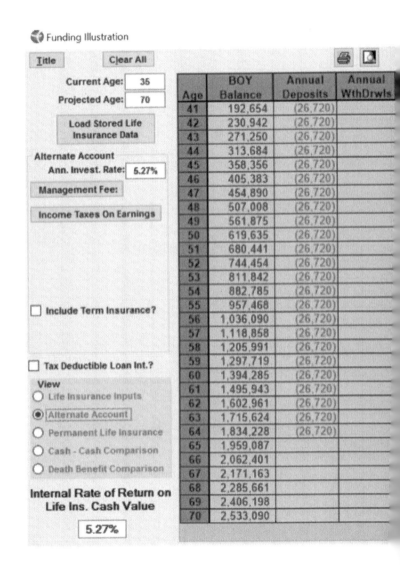

Busting the Life Insurance Lies

Annual RePmts	Annual Int. Rate	Annual Interest	EOY Balance
	5.27 %	11,569	230,942
	5.27 %	13,588	271,250
	5.27 %	15,714	313,684
	5.27 %	17,951	358,356
	5.27 %	20,307	405,383
	5.27 %	22,787	454,890
	5.27 %	25,398	507,008
	5.27 %	28,147	561,875
	5.27 %	31,040	619,635
	5.27 %	34,086	680,441
	5.27 %	37,293	744,454
	5.27 %	40,668	811,842
	5.27 %	44,222	882,786
	5.27 %	47,963	957,468
	5.27 %	51,902	1,036,090
	5.27 %	56,048	1,118,868
	5.27 %	60,413	1,205,991
	5.27 %	65,008	1,297,719
	5.27 %	69,845	1,394,285
	5.27 %	74,938	1,495,943
	5.27 %	80,299	1,602,961
	5.27 %	85,943	1,715,624
	5.27 %	91,884	1,834,228
	5.27 %	98,139	1,959,087
	5.27 %	103,314	2,062,401
	5.27 %	108,762	2,171,163
	5.27 %	114,498	2,285,661
	5.27 %	120,536	2,406,198
	5.27 %	126,893	2,533,090
	5.27 %	133,585	2,666,675

So while this policy didn't earn 5.27 in the beginning it earned more than that on the back so that it did the equivalent of 5.27 every single year, got it? When we add the tax bracket in there what we see is now this ac-

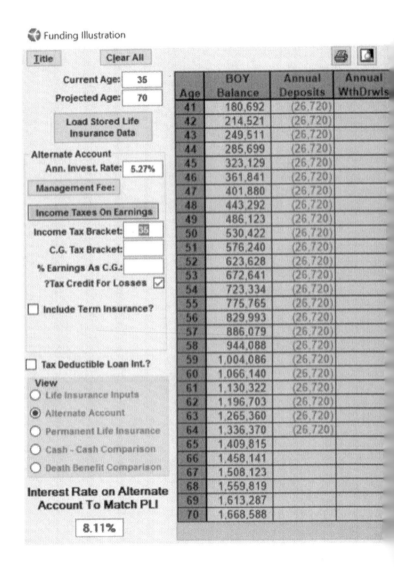

Busting the Life Insurance Lies   238

count would drop to $1,700,000. In order for it to have the same value after tax as our life insurance policy the alternate account would actually have to earn 8.11%.

Annual RePmts	Annual Int. Rate	Annual Interest	Annual Tax	EOY Balance
	5.27 %	10,938	(3,828)	214,521
	5.27 %	12,722	(4,453)	249,511
	5.27 %	14,567	(5,099)	285,699
	5.27 %	16,476	(5,766)	323,129
	5.27 %	18,450	(6,457)	361,841
	5.27 %	20,491	(7,172)	401,880
	5.27 %	22,603	(7,911)	443,292
	5.27 %	24,786	(8,675)	486,123
	5.27 %	27,045	(9,466)	530,422
	5.27 %	29,381	(10,283)	576,240
	5.27 %	31,798	(11,129)	623,628
	5.27 %	34,297	(12,004)	672,641
	5.27 %	36,881	(12,908)	723,334
	5.27 %	39,555	(13,844)	775,765
	5.27 %	42,320	(14,812)	829,993
	5.27 %	45,179	(15,813)	886,079
	5.27 %	48,137	(16,848)	944,088
	5.27 %	51,196	(17,919)	1,004,086
	5.27 %	54,360	(19,026)	1,066,140
	5.27 %	57,633	(20,172)	1,130,322
	5.27 %	61,018	(21,356)	1,196,703
	5.27 %	64,518	(22,581)	1,265,360
	5.27 %	68,139	(23,849)	1,336,370
	5.27 %	71,884	(25,159)	1,409,815
	5.27 %	74,348	(26,022)	1,458,141
	5.27 %	76,896	(26,914)	1,508,123
	5.27 %	79,532	(27,836)	1,559,819
	5.27 %	82,258	(28,790)	1,613,287
	5.27 %	85,078	(29,777)	1,668,588
	5.27 %	87,994	(30,798)	1,725,784

So while this policy didn't earn 5.27 in the beginning it earned more than that on the back so that it did the equivalent of 5.27 every single year, got it? When we add the tax bracket in there what we see is now this account would drop to $1,700,000. In order for it to have the same value after tax as our life insurance policy the alternate account would actually have to earn 8.11%.

If it did that then we would have the same amount of cash in the alternate account as we did in our savings. I don't know how many things are earning anywhere near 8.11%, forget even the liquid part. But the life insurance policy actually comes along with something called a death benefit as well, does it not? So that in the event of premature death the life insurance policy will pay to the family.

If I choose to put my money in another account, how do I protect my family in the event that I have a premature death? I'd have to buy term insurance, right? So let's add some term insurance in here. Level term insurance is where a lot of term insurance has gone. Term insurance used to be a YRP, a yearly renewable product and what would happen is it would actually increase in value a little bit each year. As you got older the increases would be larger but would continue on that curve.

Busting the Life Insurance Lies

Insurance companies came out with level term insurance and they actually dropped the premiums a little bit at a level timeframe rather than an increasing one. I would say for the insurance company's profits that's one of the most brilliant things they came up with because they passed it off on the public as a savings on insurance when in reality it guaranteed profits for the insurance companies and this is why.

In the old days, as the insurance premiums increased each year, let's say that they bought into Dave's idea of buy term invest the difference, get rid of term insurance at retirement age because you no longer have a need for it because you don't have to protect an income anymore. And your plan was to get rid of the insurance at age 65.

If that insurance was just going up, a little bit each year, and you got to age 64 you were supposed to be getting rid of your term insurance but you found out that you had a serious health issue, you might actually pay the next couple of years premium and collect on it. With a level term insurance it's $1,140 a year going down to age 64. At 65 that premium goes to $46,490. That pretty much guarantees no matter how sick this guy is he is not paying that $46,490 at that point in time to keep that term insurance alive.

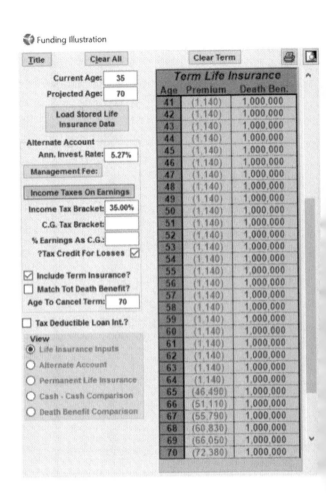

		Clear PLI			NEW	

Permanent Life Insurance

Age	Premium	Ann. Loan	Loan Int.	Loan Pmt	Net CV	Net DB
41	(26,720)				191,091	1,502,219
42	(26,720)				228,876	1,575,624
43	(26,720)				268,639	1,649,360
44	(26,720)				310,464	1,723,659
45	(26,720)				354,443	1,798,578
46	(26,720)				400,675	1,874,053
47	(26,720)				449,317	1,950,316
48	(26,720)				500,513	2,026,885
49	(26,720)				554,380	2,103,900
50	(26,720)				610,995	2,184,635
51	(26,720)				671,687	2,269,224
52	(26,720)				736,721	2,358,084
53	(26,720)				806,337	2,451,354
54	(26,720)				880,780	2,549,332
55	(26,720)				959,673	2,650,873
56	(26,720)				1,043,265	2,756,007
57	(26,720)				1,131,767	2,864,886
58	(26,720)				1,225,432	2,976,827
59	(26,720)				1,324,436	3,091,943
60	(26,720)				1,428,936	3,210,398
61	(26,720)				1,539,406	3,333,279
62	(26,720)				1,656,183	3,461,380
63	(26,720)				1,779,543	3,595,023
64	(26,720)				1,909,794	3,734,189
65					2,020,206	3,830,690
66					2,136,581	3,932,324
67					2,259,231	4,038,735
68					2,388,347	4,149,963
69					2,524,200	4,265,652
70					2,666,675	4,385,699

What does that result in? Pure profits for the insurance company and with a mutual life insurance company, it actually becomes a dividend for my cash value life insurance policy. Reality is he's not going to pay that so let's cancel the term insurance at 64.

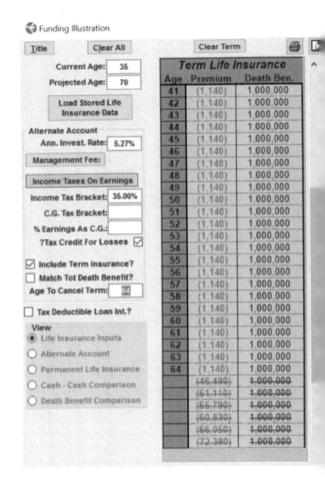

[Clear PLI] [NEW]

			Permanent Life Insurance			
Age	Premium	Ann. Loan	Loan Int.	Loan Pmt	Net CV	Net DB
41	(26,720)				191,091	1,502,219
42	(26,720)				228,876	1,575,624
43	(26,720)				268,639	1,649,360
44	(26,720)				310,464	1,723,659
45	(26,720)				354,443	1,798,578
46	(26,720)				400,675	1,874,053
47	(26,720)				449,317	1,950,316
48	(26,720)				500,513	2,026,885
49	(26,720)				554,380	2,103,900
50	(26,720)				610,995	2,184,635
51	(26,720)				671,687	2,269,224
52	(26,720)				736,721	2,358,084
53	(26,720)				806,337	2,451,354
54	(26,720)				880,780	2,549,332
55	(26,720)				959,673	2,650,873
56	(26,720)				1,043,265	2,756,007
57	(26,720)				1,131,767	2,864,886
58	(26,720)				1,225,432	2,976,827
59	(26,720)				1,324,436	3,091,943
60	(26,720)				1,428,936	3,210,398
61	(26,720)				1,539,406	3,333,279
62	(26,720)				1,656,183	3,461,380
63	(26,720)				1,779,543	3,595,023
64	(26,720)				1,909,794	3,734,189
65					2,020,206	3,830,690
66					2,136,581	3,932,324
67					2,259,231	4,038,735
68					2,388,347	4,149,963
69					2,524,200	4,265,652
70					2,666,675	4,385,699

We see it draws a line through it, since we lose the death benefit, we lose the premium at that point in time. Now think about this, this is another important part about this. What do you think your likelihood of premature death is between now and age 65 if you can get approved for the insurance from the insurance company?

Participant: Less than 1%.

Todd: Less than 1%. What do you think your chance of dying after age 64 is? It's pretty much 100%. So let's think about the logic here. With the buy term/invest the difference we are supposed to have the insurance during a timeframe that statistically not going to happen. I'm not saying don't have it because it could be the one that

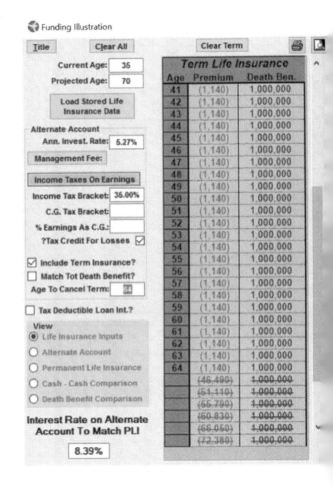

goes away but just looking at the overall picture we are supposed to get rid of it at a time when it's guaranteed to happen. Does that make sense?

And yet that's where the country has shifted because of financial planning that started occurring in the '50s. All right, so now then let's show what our return is, that's 8.39%.

		Clear PLI			N E W	
			Permanent Life Insurance			
Age	Premium	Ann. Loan	Loan Int.	Loan Pmt	Net CV	Net DB
41	(26,720)				191,091	1,502,219
42	(26,720)				228,876	1,575,624
43	(26,720)				268,639	1,649,360
44	(26,720)				310,464	1,723,659
45	(26,720)				354,443	1,798,578
46	(26,720)				400,675	1,874,053
47	(26,720)				449,317	1,950,316
48	(26,720)				500,513	2,026,885
49	(26,720)				554,380	2,103,900
50	(26,720)				610,995	2,184,635
51	(26,720)				671,687	2,269,224
52	(26,720)				736,721	2,358,084
53	(26,720)				806,337	2,451,354
54	(26,720)				880,780	2,549,332
55	(26,720)				969,673	2,650,873
56	(26,720)				1,043,265	2,756,007
57	(26,720)				1,131,767	2,864,886
58	(26,720)				1,225,432	2,976,827
59	(26,720)				1,324,436	3,091,943
60	(26,720)				1,428,936	3,210,398
61	(26,720)				1,539,406	3,333,279
62	(26,720)				1,656,183	3,461,380
63	(26,720)				1,779,543	3,595,023
64	(26,720)				1,909,794	3,734,189
65					2,020,206	3,830,690
66					2,136,581	3,932,324
67					2,259,231	4,038,735
68					2,388,347	4,149,963
69					2,524,200	4,265,652
70					2,666,675	4,385,699

What that means is we would have to earn 8.39% every single year with no down years in another account so that we could pay the taxes and term insurance that we are going to lose.

And at the end of that timeframe we'll have the same amount of cash we have in the life insurance policy.

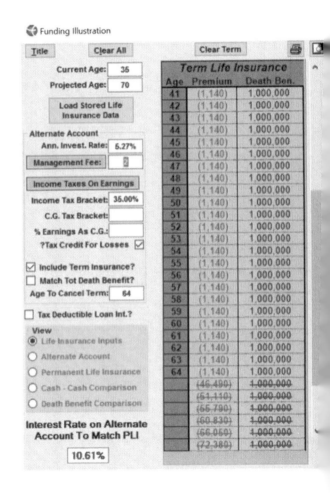

And this is supposed to have a terrible rate of return. Okay, just for fun, where could we earn 8.3%? Forget the liquidity, forget the safety, let's just see what we could do to match it. We could go to the market, couldn't we? If we do that, what's going to occur? Risks, certainly but fees, right? We are going to add the fees portion so let's add a management fee of 2%.

	Clear PLI				NEW	
		Permanent Life Insurance				
Age	Premium	Ann. Loan	Loan Int.	Loan Pmt	Net CV	Net DB
41	(26,720)				191,091	1,502,219
42	(26,720)				228,876	1,575,624
43	(26,720)				268,639	1,649,360
44	(26,720)				310,464	1,723,659
45	(26,720)				354,443	1,798,578
46	(26,720)				400,675	1,874,053
47	(26,720)				449,317	1,950,316
48	(26,720)				500,513	2,026,885
49	(26,720)				554,380	2,103,900
50	(26,720)				610,995	2,184,635
51	(26,720)				671,687	2,269,224
52	(26,720)				736,721	2,358,084
53	(26,720)				806,337	2,451,354
54	(26,720)				880,780	2,549,332
55	(26,720)				959,673	2,650,873
56	(26,720)				1,043,265	2,756,007
57	(26,720)				1,131,767	2,864,886
58	(26,720)				1,225,432	2,976,827
59	(26,720)				1,324,436	3,091,943
60	(26,720)				1,428,936	3,210,398
61	(26,720)				1,539,406	3,333,279
62	(26,720)				1,656,183	3,461,380
63	(26,720)				1,779,543	3,595,023
64	(26,720)				1,909,794	3,734,189
65					2,020,206	3,830,690
66					2,136,581	3,932,324
67					2,259,231	4,038,735
68					2,388,347	4,149,963
69					2,524,200	4,265,652
70					2,666,675	4,385,699

Now we'd have to earn 10.61% every year on a mutual fund, no down years. We can't earn an average 10.6%, we have to earn an actual 10.6% and if we do that all we are going to have is the same amount of cash but we are not going to have this extra $2 million of death benefit here. Does that make sense? Are we talking about maximums here or minimums?

Participant: Minimums.

Todd: Minimums, why?

Participants: Because it's an "and" product.

Todd: Because it's an "and" product. This assumes that we parked our money in here and never touched it. We didn't take advantage of helping our child or grandchild with the credit card debt they had and making additional money on the side and helping them as well. We didn't take advantage of the real estate deal that comes along.

We didn't take advantage of any of those things we might be able to do with our financing in other places. And yet even with that that's what the equivalent yield is. It's not to say that's the internal rate of return on life insurance policy and notice the wording changed to interest rate on alternate account to match the PLI. That's what it takes in order for it to have the same amount of money at the end of that timeframe, any questions on that?

Participant: Ignoring the leverage of death benefit.

Todd: Ignoring the leverage of death benefit, absolutely. Just to add to what you are saying about the leverage of death benefit, think about this, if you knew in the future maybe even when you are dead that you are going to have an extra $2 million that's going to fall into your estate, would that change how you could spend money today?

Busting the Life Insurance Lies

This impacts our ability to change the way we spend dollars today. Everybody looks at, well the death benefit is going to be a benefit to our kids, our grandkids or whatever. No, that's a benefit to us today because knowing that that's coming in, in the future changes what I can do with my money now between now and then because that's a guaranteed event, both of them.

We've got a guarantee of death and we've got a guarantee of life insurance being paid. Those two together allow us to leverage the way we spend money today, yes or no? Absolutely. This is a stout policy, the returns on this one are high, there's no question. But again, it's real.

Kim: Based on today's numbers.

Todd: Based on today's numbers but this is an aggressive illustrator. There's no question. But again, the reason I use this is because we are making comparisons and that's what we are forced to do in our industry against the last 25 years in the market. That's what we are comparing against. It's not a fair comparison because we are going from today. So I'm going to take the most aggressive thing I can find in this case and that's what we've done.

Participant: I agree. I mean, is there any way to put the real estate return that we enjoy from the cash value of that life insurance policy over and over and over and over for the next 28 years?

Todd: Right. And for the previous 28, they are using those numbers to project into the future. That means the market has to do that which means the economy has improved, which means the dividends improved even if the money just sat there.

Let's understand something. I know a lot of you think well I've reached an older age now it doesn't work for me anymore. The thing about it is life insurance is designed to work over a long period of time. If I take a 50-year old out at 65, will that policy perform as well as this 35-year old out at 65? No, because this one had 30 years to get there versus 10.

The difference in age, as long as health is not a big factor, doesn't radically influence the return on the policies over the same time frame. Does that make sense? Is the premium higher? Yes. Guess what that does? It makes the cash value higher. It's not a bad thing that the premium is higher. The returns are similar.

We want to remember we haven't used the money at all in the life insurance contract to take advantage of the opportunities that might come along.

People should be lined up around the block to buy this stuff from you if they could just understand it for what it is. We don't have to make it into more than what it is, we just have to explain it for what it is. The insurance company when you call them they ought to say, you know what, we ran out. Give us until next week and we'll get some more. (laughter)

How do you beat this? And it's not supposed to compete here. It's a savings vehicle that's liquid, that we have access to, that's safe. It shouldn't be competing with investment assets and yet it can. It's pretty phenomenal and it gets even better when we use those dollars when an opportunity comes along.

Busting the Life Insurance Lies

Kim D. H. Butler and Jack Burns

Acknowledgments

I feel very fortunate to have been part of writing this book. I'd first like to acknowledge my co-author, Kim Butler. Kim is one of the best in the business, and getting to share in her knowledge, experience, and passion during this writing process has been a great pleasure. I also want to thank James Ranson and the rest of the Master Wordsmith team for their excellent work in making this book a reality.

My dad was one of the greatest men I have ever known. Most of what I know in business and in life, I learned from him. I was blessed to spend the last years of his life working alongside him and my brother Dan in our family business. After he passed, it was Dan's and my honor to build that business to a level of success we knew would make our Dad even prouder. Dan is not just my brother, he's my best friend, and I want to thank both him and our dad for the privilege of sharing that experience with them.

My mom is one of the toughest people I know. She is the glue that held our family together and without her I know I wouldn't be where I am today. She's the one who should really be writing a book--her life's stories are way more interesting than mine! To my sisters, Mary Beth, Sheila, and Amy: I know how easily a family business can tear a family apart, and I thank each of you for helping keep ours together.

Finally and most importantly, I want to thank God and my own family: Lori, John, James, and Annie. Family is the thread of all my success, and I am truly blessed and grateful for their faith, their support, and their belief in me.

Busting the Life Insurance Lies

I hope this book helps answer any questions you have about life insurance and its role in your personal investment strategy. My unique business background has provided me with almost every imaginable situation in which life insurance can be used as a vehicle to enhance wealth and give incredible security at the same time. I hope you find something here that helps you on your own road to financial success.

—*Jack Burns*

***

When Jack first mentioned wanting to co-write a book, I was immediately grateful because I wanted the help! Many people ask how I get the books done, and my answer is "It is ALWAYS a team!" This time the team included Jack, the wonderful Master Wordsmith team led by James Ranson, and editing genius Kate Phillips. It was fun to listen to James interview Jack and then see the story come together into something we're proud of. I hope you enjoy reading it!

I too am very faith-oriented and am so grateful to God everyday that my husband Todd Langford (of TruthConcepts.com) and I get to share the role of helping financial advisors nationwide tell the whole truth about all things financial. Todd's son Jake created a quote I just love: "the keeper of a truth still has to pursue it." Todd and I get to do that every day in many aspects of life.

I am also grateful to each of our clients at clients at Partners for Prosperity because they are the ones that came up with these Life Insurance Lies we made an effort to Bust so that readers (which I am also grateful to) will have a chance to learn the whole truth. Keep up your good questions and reach out to either of us to get them answered!

—*Kim Butler*

About the Authors

Kim D. H. Butler is a leader in the Prosperity Economics Movement, which offers an alternative to "typical" financial planning and its tendency to subject assets to never-ending taxes, fees, and market risk. She is an oft-interviewed expert on creative whole life insurance strategies and alternative investments such as life settlements and bridge loans. Described as a "financial rule-breaker," Kim is an educator and advocate as well as an advisor, and she continues to educate other advisors along with clients.

After several successful years in banking and financial planning, Kim grew disillusioned with those industries, realizing that much of their structure and practices were misleading and harmful. Driven to find a better way to provide financial counsel, Kim studied the commonalities and best practices between wealth builders across the board, eventually compiling her observations into the 7 Principles of Prosperity, which later became a foundational piece of the Prosperity Economics Movement.

In 1999, Kim left an established financial planning company and founded Partners for Prosperity, LLC, a financial advising and life insurance business dedicated to the prosperity principles she compiled. She and her husband, Todd Langford, developed The Summit for Prosperity Economics Advisors, which they host regularly around the US. She also assists Langford in training Truth Concepts Software, which is used by agents, advisors, and other financial professionals to show the "whole truth" about financial strategies.

Kim's work has been recommended by financial thought leaders and authors such as Robert Kiyosaki *(Rich Dad, Poor Dad);* Tom Dyson, publisher of the Palm Beach Letter investment newsletter; Tom Wheelright *(Tax Free Wealth)*; and Garret Gunderson *(Killing Sacred Cows)*. Her previous books include *Busting the Financial Planning Lies, Busting the Retirement Lies, Busting the Interest Rate Lies,* and the Amazon bestseller *Live Your Life Insurance.*

When Kim isn't busy strategizing with her clients or helping other advisors, she puts her energy to good use by enjoying time with her family, hiking, working on their East Texas alpaca farm, and reading with Emma, the Great Dane (Kim reads, Emma sleeps).

***

Jack Burns is the owner of JB Life, a client-focused investment company specializing in wealth building strategies designed around its clients' specific needs. Jack has a degree in business, is a licensed insurance agent in all 50 states and is a member of numerous insurance and investment organizations across the country.

He has over 30 years of extensive experience in insurance, investment, sales and business.

In early 1990, after several years of being an insurance agent, Jack started his own regional general insurance agency. Over a decade, he built it into the top-ranked agency for his company before he left in 2001 to join his family's AG Construction business. Over the next 15 years, he and his brother Dan worked to grow the business to nearly $100 million in sales nationwide with about 200 employees. The family sold the business in September 2015 to a private equity company.

Feeling he was too young to retire and with a sincere desire to help people succeed financially, he decided to get back into the business that he was truly passionate about. Using his vast insurance and business experience, Jack wants to provide guidance to others who want to grow their business or personal wealth into having unlimited potential.

Jack and his wife Lori have been married for 25 years. They live in Iowa with their 3 children: John, James, and Annie.

***

James Ranson's recent path has led him from academic writing to arts administration to freelance editing and ghostwriting to professional speaking and authorship. After spending about 20 years taking unhelpful and unhealthy shortcuts in business and life, James decided to start playing the long game rather than looking for the next quick fix, and built a six-figure book creation business within the following 12 months. That business, The Master Wordsmith LLC, is dedicated to helping business leaders, entrepreneurs, and speakers create and publish masterpiece books without taking costly shortcuts. Members of The Master Wordsmith team have collectively co-written, edited, designed, narrated, and/or launched over 150 books.

James is a Wall Street Journal bestselling editor and has done editing and ghostwriting work for a number of book creation companies, including Tucker Max's Book In A Box and Tyler Wagner's Authors Unite. James has edited articles for *The Huffington Post* and *Good Men Project*, written grants for three opera companies, coached speakers for four TEDx events, spent a year on a road trip around the US and Central America, and sung in Carnegie Hall. His first book, *Buy Once, Cry Once: How Shortcuts Cost You In The Long Run*, will be published in fall 2016. A graduate of Carnegie Mellon University, he divides his time between St. Louis, MO, and further road trips.

Connect with James at www.themasterwordsmith.com.

About The Prosperity Economics Movement

Before the rise of today's financial planning industry and its focus on market-based retirement planning, people built wealth over time with diligence, common sense, and a long-term view. Instead of creating ever-changing stock portfolios and restrictive 401(k) plans, investors built equity through property ownership, business development, and dividend-paying whole life insurance. "Financial planning" as we know it today was the exception, not the rule.

Here's the thing: most wealthy people today still build their wealth exactly the same way, using principles we like to call "Prosperity Economics." It's usually only the rest of us—busy, uninformed, confused, and new to investing—that don't follow these time-tested practices for building real wealth. Why? Partially because we don't know any better, but mostly, because we're never taught Prosperity Economics.

Instead, we are steered away from proven, traditional methods of creating wealth, and directed to become buyers of a puzzling maze of complicated financial instruments and vehicles that don't even make sense to the people who sell them. Mutual funds have become so intricate that even explaining how they work is practically impossible, let alone predicting when they'll make or lose money. And as if that weren't bad enough, over 30% of the average investor's hard-earned money gets siphoned off in administration and management fees—paid to financial advisors who often have conflicts of interest.

Prosperity Economics reintroduces traditional and trusted ways to grow and protect your money reliably and sustainably. Prosperity Economics is an alternative to "typical" financial planning that shows you how to control your own wealth instead of trusting your financial security and growth to conflicted corporations, complex government oversight, and fickle market forces.

Now, typical financial planning is better than nothing. But we believe that you, no matter how much or little you know about investing or money management, can do a lot better. This is why we created the Prosperity Economics Movement. This movement is actually comprised of smaller movements that represent alternatives to a financial planning industry we believe has gone off course. You may have heard of The Infinite Banking Concept, Private or Family Banking, Rich Dad Strategies, Circle of Wealth, or Bank on Yourself. Advisors and agents within the movement may use different language and even suggest different financial strategies, but they honor a common set of principles, such as the 7 Principles of Prosperity™ articulated by Kim Butler.

The Prosperity Economics Movement (PEM) has two websites, ProsperityPeaks.com for American investors and consumers, and ProsperityEconomicsAdvisors.com for advisors and other financial professionals. Prosperity Peaks helps people like you discover how you can take back control of your thinking and your finances. Prosperity Economics Advisors is a community that helps insurance advisors develop a prosperity mindset and learn the best ways to help their clients achieve long-term financial success.

IMPLEMENTING PROSPERITY ECONOMICS

With Prosperity Economics, wealth isn't measured by how much money you have, but by how much freedom you have with your money. We focus on reliable, real-time cash flow rather than a far-off net worth number that you can never use to improve your life. Our priorities are liquidity, control, and safety, not gambling on a high rate of return you may never see. (See the diagram below for some key differences between Prosperity Economics and "typical" financial planning.)

Prosperity Economics gives you the flexibility to live your unique life to the fullest, along with the reliable cash flow to support whatever kind of life you choose yours to be—in other words, to reach your financial peaks.

To explore your new financial strategy, we invite you to book a complimentary conversation with Kim, Jack, or another Prosperity Economics advisor. In this meeting, we will get to know you and your unique situation, discuss your personal financial goals, and answer questions about how to get your money working for you, rather than the other way around. In particular, we'll examine cash storage, asset growth, and income, the three main areas of interest for people looking to improve their finances.

We'll show you some of the ways to improve your cash flow and create a more reliable financial system for yourself—without taking big risks, paying unnecessary taxes, or sapping your fiscal growth with stacks of management fees. We'll likely suggest alternative approaches to the typical financial planning of today's industry, and we can propose effective debt solutions if needed.

Every strategy we suggest is proven in our own and our clients' experience. Our cash strategy grows cash many times faster than typical bank CD rates, while defer¬ring taxes and offering other benefits. Our stock market alternative (especially effective for accredited investors) is not affected by stock market condi-tions, interest rates, or politics. We can even suggest alternatives to bonds or annuities for cash flow that offer more attractive rates without requiring a long-term surrender of assets.

Busting the Life Insurance Lies

To find out more or book your complimentary conversation, visit ProsperityPeaks.com, or contact us directly: Kim@Partners4Prosperity.com , or Jack@JBLife.com.

FINANCIAL PLANNING	VS.	PROSPERITY ECONOMICS
Meets needs and goals only		**Pursues wants and dreams**
Based on limited ideas of "what you can afford."		Based on unlimited ideas of "what is possible?"
Minimizes requirements		**Optimizes opportunities**
"How much do I have to save?"		"How else can I build wealth?" mindset.
Product-oriented (what you buy)		**Strategy-oriented (what you do)**
Focus is primarily on buying certain products.		Based on time-tested principles and financial philosophies used to build wealth.
Focused on rate-of-return		**Focused on recovering opportunity cost**
"How much is this earning me?"		Keep more money working for you.
Institutions control your money		**You control your money**
Put your assets "under management," (and/or give control to government.)		Maintain responsibility for and access to your assets and funds.
Micro (vacuum) based		**Macro (big picture) based**
Focus is on your "portfolio."		View your whole personal economy.
Net worth is measurement		**Cash flow is measurement**
A bigger portfolio is the goal.		The goal is more money to enjoy each month.
Retirement oriented		**Abundant/Freedom orientated**
Your reward for work is not working.		Enjoy your work and your life – all life long.
Lives only on interest		
At mercy of interest rates, with fingers crossed you won't need to use principle.		**Spends and replaces principle**
Money stays still		A flexible, sustainable way to live.
Assets are accumulated into accounts where they sit, financially "stagnant."		**Money moves**
		Your personal economy is alive and well, money flows in and out of account.
Dollars do only one job		**Dollars do many jobs**
Save separately for emergencies, education, retirement, major purchases. Spend each dollar for one purpose only.		Dollars are used for flexible and multiple purposes.
Professional planner is the expert		**Clients are empowered**
Finances are represented as something confusing that should be delegated.		Money is demystified. Education-based approach builds financial confidence.

PROSPERITY ECONOMICS ADVISORS

Prosperity Economics Advisors represents the advisor side of the Prosperity Economics Movement, comprised of financial professionals who are tired of the "max out your 401(k) and hope for the best" or "dump everything into mutual funds and let the broker handle everything" messages both they and their clients run into these days. If you're an insurance advisor or financial planner, and you like the message and content of this book, we invite you to find out more at ProsperityEconomicsAdvisors.com.

Our goal is to connect advisors like you across the country (and beyond!) who are using or interested in learning about Prosperity Economics and the 7 Principles of Prosperity™, so we don't all have to work in isolation anymore. We prefer preparation over planning, protection over risk tolerance, creation over consumption, and prosperity over scarcity. We believe in seeking out the whole truth about financial decisions, using our talents, strengths, and experiences to help others, teaching those who would learn from us how to apply the principles of prosperity to their own lives, and ultimately, guiding our nation and our world onto more solid economic footing.

If this sounds like a community you'd like to be part of, visit us at ProsperityEconomicsAdvisors.com and sign up to receive your copy of Kim Butler's Prosperity Economics "manifesto," Financial Planning Has Failed. In addition to the ebook, you'll get periodic tips on how best to help your clients, information about online trainings as well as our annual Summit of prosperity-minded financial professionals, invitations to learn more about the award-winning Truth Concepts financial software, and more.

Join this forward-looking community by signing up at ProsperityEconomicsAdvisors.com. We look forward to connecting with you!

Busting the Life Insurance Lies

Book a Prosperity Economics Speaker for Your Next Event!

For General Audiences

Throughout the country, Prosperity Economics spokespersons are available to speak about Prosperity Economics, along with related financial topics.

Are you looking for a particular subject area? Perhaps your audience would like to learn:

- Retirement plan realities—why qualified plans don't perform as illustrated

- How to save without the risks and roller coaster of the stock market

- Qualified plan alternatives that can significantly reduce future taxes

- The impact of inflation and the danger of retiring too soon

- Saving enough? Why most of us need to save more!

- Financial Planning versus Prosperity Economics

Speakers for Advisor Conferences

Author Kim Butler and Truth Concepts founder Todd Langford are available to speak to advisors or agents about Prosperity Economics, including a Truth Concepts demo that uses calculators and tools to illustrate some of the distinctions of Prosperity Economics. (Truth Concepts is financial software dedicated to telling the whole truth about money. It's built for advisors yet available to anyone at Truth-Concepts.com.)

This eye-opening half-day presentation takes advisors on a fascinating journey through various financial philosophies and concepts, ultimately teaching them how to talk about and illustrate a broad range of financial strategies with clients. Contact Kim@Partners-4Prosperity.com for details.

Truth Training

Langford and Butler also conduct seminars several times a year for advisors (anyone is welcome) on using Truth Concepts software. Purchase of the software is not necessary, any advisor can benefit, and some find it so beneficial they return again and again! For more information, visit TruthConcepts.com.

Kim D. H. Butler and Jack Burns

Also by Kim D. H. Butler:

Busting the Interest Rate Lies: Discover the Whole Truth About Money and How You Can Keep Control of Yours
(Available on Amazon.com or at ProsperityPeaks.com)

Live Your Life Insurance: Surprising Strategies to Build Lifelong Prosperity with Your Whole Life Policy
(Available on Amazon.com or at LiveYourLifeInsurance.com)

Busting the Financial Planning Lies: Learn to Use Prosperity Economics to Build Sustainable Wealth
(Available on Amazon.com or ProsperityPeaks.com)

Busting the Retirement Lies: Living with Passion, Purpose, and Abundance Throughout Our Lives
(Available on Amazon.com or ProsperityPeaks.com)

PRAISE FOR *BUSTING THE INTEREST RATE LIES*

"Amazing proof about 30 year mortgages being more effective than 15 year mortgages."

Tim Barnett
President, America's Mortgage Center, Ltd.

"Kim's newest book contains a great story on using life insurance and investment real estate together."

Tom Dyson
Publisher, Palm Beach Research Group

"Investment education, some for the masses, some for the millionaires."

Todd Strobel
"No BS Money Guy"

"This is a must-have book in every household in America. Getting your best negotiated price on a purchase of automobiles, equipment, rental properties, personal residence, and paying for education is only a small piece of the cost. This book is a major piece to your purchasing decisions!"

Tim Cooper, CRFA
Ripple Effect Investment Strategies, LLC

PRAISE FOR *LIVE YOUR LIFE INSURANCE*

"This is the way to look at life insurance. Kim Butler has a unique and refreshing view of life insurance. Instead of only receiving benefit from your insurance when you die, she explains how... life insurance can be an asset throughout your life. I am also one of Kim's clients, and I can honestly say that insurance as she explains it works just like she says it does in *Live Your Life Insurance*. **A great book and a new way of thinking** about life insurance that everyone should read."

Tom Wheelwright, CPA
Author of Tax-Free Wealth

"Very useful book. Kim Butler... clearly presents you with the little-known fact that "the first Beneficiary of your Life Insurance policy should be YOU. I've known of Kim for years, and I've verified these concepts over the last 25+ years, even longer than I've known her. This is an excellent, common-sense approach to personal finance, and it could not come at a better time."

Bobby Mattei
R.S. Mattei & Associates

"The heart of the matter. One would be hard pressed to find another person on the planet with more working knowledge of the power of whole life insurance and the plethora of uses for this most underappreciated and often abused financial tool than Kim Butler.

Life insurance, properly structured and utilized is without a doubt THE most potent financial tool to create wealth for families, business owners and individuals... Kim's book is a welcome addition to the increasing clamor for accurate, viable information for those wanting to create, use and maintain wealth without resorting to the gambling in the markets."

Jim Kindred
Financial Strategies Group

PRAISE FOR *BUSTING THE RETIREMENT LIES*

"Fantastic Guide for Re-thinking Retirement! This book crunches some serious numbers with screen-captured financial software (you'll be appalled to learn the toll that taxes and fees take on "your" money), but it's about SO much more than financial strategies. Butler tackles the very IDEA of retirement and offers alternatives, along with many case studies and examples of people who are doing things differently. While sobering at times, it's **ultimately an inspiring read that gives many practical tips for creating a fulfilling and prosperous life at any age."**

Kathy Pritchard
Financial Coach

"Great Read. I am 73 and semi-retired (work part time to keep busy and I love my job.) Wish I read her books years ago. **Never too late to learn and improve your financial situation."**

Jesse C. Spriggs
Amazon Reviewer

"Five Stars. It is about time someone wrote this book. Thanks, Kim. Read and learn the truth!"

Mary Barrett
Amazon reviewer

"Busting the Retirement Lies makes a compelling argument that we've been thinking about aging all wrong... and not just financially speaking."

R. Nelson Nash
Author of *Becoming Your Own Banker*

Made in the USA
Middletown, DE
24 August 2018